STRATEGIES FOR BUILDING STRONGER RELATIONSHIPS

# DIG DEEP BEFORE YOU LEAP

## THE ULTIMATE RELATIONSHIP WORKBOOK FOR SINGLES

Your Relationship Workbook to Identify
Red Flags, Deal Breakers, and Warning Signs

## CL. REDDON

# COPYRIGHT DISCLAIMER

**Copyright © 2023 by CL. Reddon**

# ABOUT CL. REDDON

CL. Reddon is a communications strategist, author, speaker, and coach. His signature messages of transformation are known for their warmth, wisdom, and humor. He dedicates much of his time to his work, writing books that help people achieve maximum success by sharing the power of perseverance, reinvention, transformation, and evolution.

As the author of "Dig Deep Before You Leap: Critical Factors To Explore Before Engaging In Marriage," CL. Reddon has made it his mission to help people make informed decisions about their romantic relationships. His coaching and writing are grounded in research-based principles and strategies, making them effective tools for anyone seeking to build a lasting and meaningful relationship.

# CONTENTS

# DIG DEEP BEFORE YOU LEAP

# DEDICATION

My sincere thanks are extended to all the single women and men who are reading this book. Finding love and romance can be a challenging journey, but you are not alone in this endeavor. I admire your courage and perseverance in your pursuit of finding your soulmate.

Remember that being single is not a curse, and it is a valuable time to grow and discover yourself. It is essential to take care of yourself and love yourself first before searching for a partner.

This book is for you, to provide you with the tools and knowledge necessary to navigate the complex world of dating and relationships. I hope it helps you find clarity, confidence, and ultimately, the love and romance you deserve.

Always keep an open mind and a positive outlook, and never forget that you are worthy of love and happiness.

Best of luck on your journey!

*C. L. Reddon*

# INTRODUCTION

Relationships are a beautiful and complex experience that can bring immense joy, love, and connection. However, they can also be challenging and frustrating, filled with conflict, misunderstandings, and heartbreak. In today's society, where we are more connected than ever, finding and maintaining a healthy relationship has become increasingly difficult.

With the rise of social media and dating apps, we have more options than ever before, but these tools also make it easier to fall into patterns of instant gratification, superficial connections, and unrealistic expectations. The lack of in-person communication and the prevalence of ghosting and breadcrumbing can leave us feeling disheartened and hopeless.

That's why dedicated tools and guidance in the art of relationships are more necessary than ever before. This workbook provides valuable insights, practical advice, and exercises to help you navigate the ups and downs of relationships. It will help you build healthy communication skills, set boundaries, and develop a deeper understanding of yourself and your partner.

My goal in this workbook is to guide you in exploring the critical factors that you should consider before entering into a marriage. We'll dive deep into topics such as identifying red flags in relationships, setting healthy boundaries, and effectively communicating with your partner.

I believe that taking the time to explore these factors is crucial to building a strong and healthy relationship. That's why this workbook is designed to help you gain the skills and knowledge you need to make informed decisions about your romantic relationships.

Together, we'll also examine the importance of premarital research, investigating your partner's background, and understanding the role of good credit in committed relationships. By the end of this workbook, you will be well-equipped to make wise choices about your romantic partnerships, setting yourself up for success in your future relationships.

Whether you are single and looking for love or already in a relationship, this workbook is an invaluable resource for anyone who wants to improve their relationships and live a happier, more fulfilling life.

So, are you ready to dig deep and explore the critical factors to consider before engaging in marriage? Let's get started!

# Dysfunctional Relationship Danger

# What Are Red Flags in Relationships?

Relationships are an essential part of our lives, and they play a significant role in our mental, emotional, and physical well-being. However, not all relationships are healthy or positive. Sometimes, we may find ourselves in relationships that are toxic or abusive, and it can be challenging to identify these warning signs before it's too late. These warning signs, commonly known as red flags, can help us recognize potentially harmful relationships and take the necessary steps to protect ourselves.

Red flags can manifest in many ways, and they can vary depending on the type of relationship and the individuals involved. However, some common red flags include:

1. Control Issues: A partner who tries to control or manipulate you, your actions, or your decisions is a significant red flag. This can manifest in many ways, such as trying to isolate you from your friends and family, monitoring your every move, or dictating how you should dress, behave, or speak.

2. Lack of Empathy: Empathy is an essential part of any healthy relationship. If your partner consistently dismisses your feelings, belittles your emotions, or fails to take your perspective into account, it could be a sign of a lack of empathy.

3. Disrespectful or Aggressive Behavior: Any form of physical or emotional abuse is a major red flag in a relationship. This can include verbal abuse, physical violence, or sexual assault. It's important to recognize that abuse can take many forms and can often be subtle, so it's essential to pay attention to any behavior that makes you feel uncomfortable or unsafe.

4. Dishonesty: Trust is a crucial component of any healthy relationship. If your partner lies to you, keeps secrets, or withholds information, it can erode the foundation of trust and lead to further problems in the relationship.

5.  Incompatibility: While it's natural to have some differences in a relationship, major differences in core values, goals, or beliefs can be a red flag. It's essential to recognize when these differences cannot be reconciled and may lead to significant problems down the road.

Recognizing red flags in a relationship can be challenging, particularly when we are emotionally invested in the relationship. However, it's essential to take these warning signs seriously and to take action when necessary. Here are some steps you can take if you notice red flags in your relationship:

1.  Talk to your partner: If you notice red flags in your relationship, it's important to have an open and honest conversation with your partner. Be clear about your concerns and listen to their perspective. If your partner is willing to work on the issues and make positive changes, it may be possible to salvage the relationship.

2.  Seek support: Talking to a trusted friend or family member can be helpful in gaining perspective on the situation. Additionally, seeking the help of a therapist or counselor can provide a safe and supportive space to explore your feelings and options.

3.  Take action: If your partner is unwilling or unable to make positive changes, it may be necessary to take action to protect yourself. This can include ending the relationship, seeking legal protection, or seeking the help of a domestic violence hotline.

Recognizing red flags in a relationship is essential to protecting our mental, emotional, and physical well-being. While these warning signs can be difficult to recognize, paying attention to our instincts and seeking support, when necessary, can help us make healthy and positive decisions for ourselves. If you notice red flags in your relationship, remember that you deserve to be treated with respect and kindness, and it's never too late to make a change.

# Why Are Red Flags Important?

Recognizing red flags in a relationship is crucial for several reasons. Firstly, red flags can indicate potential issues that may cause problems in the future. By identifying and addressing these warning signs early on, you can work together with your partner to address any underlying issues and improve the health of your relationship.

Secondly, ignoring red flags can lead to serious problems in a relationship. If warning signs are ignored or overlooked, they may escalate and become more difficult to address over time. This can lead to feelings of frustration, resentment, and ultimately the breakdown of the relationship.

Thirdly, identifying and addressing red flags can help you make informed decisions about the future of your relationship. By being aware of potential issues, you can make a more informed decision about whether or not to continue with the relationship.

Ray and Nicole have been dating for six months. At first, everything seemed perfect. Ray was attentive and affectionate, and Nicole felt like she had finally found someone who understood her. However, over the past few weeks, Nicole has noticed some red flags in their relationship. Ray has become increasingly jealous and controlling, often checking her phone and getting upset when she spends time with her friends without him. Nicole is starting to feel like she can't do anything without Ray's approval and she's worried that things will only get worse.

*Tips:*

1. Trust your instincts - if something doesn't feel right in your relationship, don't ignore it. Trust your gut and take action to address any concerns that you may have.

2. Communicate openly and honestly - if you're experiencing red flags in your relationship, it's important to communicate your concerns with your partner. Be clear about what you're experiencing and how it's making you feel.

3. Set boundaries - if your partner is exhibiting controlling or jealous behavior, it's important to set boundaries and make it clear what you are and aren't comfortable with in the relationship.

4. Seek support - if you're struggling to address red flags in your relationship, don't hesitate to seek support from friends, family, or a therapist. Talking to someone can help you gain clarity and find the courage to take action.

5. Remember that you deserve to be treated with respect - if your partner is exhibiting red flags, it's important to remember that you deserve to be treated with respect and dignity in your relationship. Don't settle for anything less than you deserve.

**Summary**

Red flags are important to recognize because they can indicate potential issues in a relationship, ignoring them can lead to serious problems, and being aware of them can help you make more informed decisions about the future of your relationship. It is important to pay attention to warning signs and to address any concerns that you may have with your partner openly and honestly.

**Knowledge Check**

We have now completed Section A, and it is time to take a knowledge test to evaluate your understanding and knowledge of the topics covered.

*True or False:*

1. Red flags are behaviors or actions that can indicate potential problems in a relationship.

2. Red flags are always obvious and easy to spot.

3.  One red flag in a relationship means that the relationship is unhealthy.

4.  Red flags may develop gradually over time.

5.  Communication is not important when it comes to addressing red flags in a relationship.

6.  Ignoring red flags can lead to serious problems in a relationship.

7.  Addressing red flags in a relationship can help you make more informed decisions about the future of the relationship.

8.  It's important to trust your instincts if something doesn't feel right in a relationship.

9.  Seeking support from friends, family, or a therapist can be helpful if you're experiencing red flags in a relationship.

10. You should settle for less than you deserve in a relationship if red flags are present.

*Fill in the blank:*

1.  Red flags are behaviors or actions that can indicate potential ___________ in a relationship.

2.  It is important to communicate ___________ and honestly with your partner about any red flags in your relationship.

3.  Ignoring red flags can lead to serious ___________ in a relationship.

4.  Trusting your ___________ is important when it comes to addressing red flags in a relationship.

5.  Setting ___________ can help address controlling or jealous behavior in a relationship.

6. Seeking support from a therapist or counselor can be helpful if you're experiencing _________ in a relationship.

7. Red flags may be _________ or disguised as seemingly harmless behavior.

8. Recognizing red flags can help you make more _________ decisions about the future of your relationship.

9. Lack of _________ is a common red flag in unhealthy relationships.

10. Respecting each other's _________ is an important aspect of a healthy relationship.

## Communication Red Flags

Communication is the foundation of any healthy relationship, and effective communication is key to maintaining a strong connection with your partner. However, certain communication patterns can be red flags that may indicate potential problems in a relationship. Some common communication red flags include stonewalling, defensiveness, disrespectful language, and avoiding communication. If you notice any of these patterns in your relationship, it's important to address them with your partner and work together to find healthier ways to communicate.

Stonewalling involves refusing to engage in a conversation or shutting down emotionally during a discussion. This can be frustrating for your partner and can make it difficult to resolve conflicts. Defensiveness involves becoming defensive or blaming your partner when they bring up concerns or criticisms. This can create a cycle of negative communication and make it difficult to find common ground. Disrespectful language, such as name-calling or belittling, can be hurtful and damaging to a relationship. Avoiding communication altogether can be just as harmful, as it can prevent you and your partner from resolving issues and growing closer.

If you notice any of these communication patterns in your relationship, it's important to address them with your partner. Take time to reflect on your own communication style and identify ways that you can improve. Work together with your partner to find healthy ways to communicate and resolve conflicts. This may involve seeking the help of a therapist or counselor.

## Trust Red Flags

Trust is an essential component of a healthy relationship, and a lack of trust can be a major red flag. Some common trust red flags include being overly controlling, accusing your partner of cheating without evidence, checking your partner's phone or email without permission, and lying. These behaviors can be harmful and damaging to a relationship, and they can erode the trust that is necessary for a strong connection.

Janet had been dating Phil for several months and things were going well at first. However, she started noticing some red flags that made her uncomfortable. Phil would frequently criticize her appearance, belittle her opinions, and isolate her from her friends and family. Janet began to feel trapped and unsure of what to do.

To protect herself, Janet should take the following steps:

1. Trust her instincts: If something feels off in the relationship, Janet should trust her instincts and pay attention to red flags.

2. Communicate her concerns: Janet should talk to Phil about the behaviors that are making her uncomfortable. She should use "I" statements and be clear about how his actions are affecting her.

3. Set boundaries: Janet should be clear about her expectations and establish boundaries to protect herself from harmful behavior.

4. Seek support: Janet should reach out to friends, family, or a therapist for support and guidance.

5. End the relationship if necessary: If Phil's behavior doesn't improve, Janet should consider ending the relationship to protect herself from further harm.

By taking these steps, Janet can protect herself from the red flags in her relationship and ensure her own safety and well-being. If you notice any of these trust red flags in your relationship, it's important to address them with your partner. Take time to reflect on why you may be feeling insecure or mistrustful, and work with your partner to rebuild trust. This may involve setting boundaries and establishing clear communication, seeking the help of a therapist or counselor, and taking concrete steps to regain your partner's trust.

## Emotional Red Flags

Emotional red flags can be indicators of potential problems in a relationship. Some common emotional red flags include extreme jealousy, constant criticism, emotional abuse, and gaslighting. These behaviors can be harmful and damaging to a relationship, and they can erode the emotional connection that is necessary for a strong partnership.

If you notice any of these emotional red flags in your relationship, it's important to seek help from a therapist or counselor. Take time to reflect on why you may be experiencing these emotions, and work with your partner to address the situation. This may involve setting boundaries and establishing clear communication, seeking support from a therapist or counselor, and taking steps to protect yourself from further harm.

## Physical Red Flags

Physical red flags can be serious indicators of potential problems in a relationship. Some common physical red flags include physical violence, sexual abuse, controlling behavior, and stalking. These behaviors can be dangerous and can put your safety at risk. Let's look at an example.

Dan and Tonya have been dating for a few months, and things have been going well. However, Tonya has started to notice some concerning behavior from Dan. He often gets jealous and possessive, and he's started to become more physical with her. He'll grab her arm tightly when he's angry or push her during an argument. Tonya is starting to feel scared and doesn't know what to do.

To protect herself, Tonya should take the following steps:

1. Take the red flags seriously: Physical violence is never okay, and Tonya should not brush off Dan's behavior as just being "passionate" or "jealous". She should trust her instincts and take any threats or signs of violence seriously.

2. Establish boundaries: Tonya should clearly communicate her boundaries to Dan. For example, she could say something like, "It's not okay to grab me or push me when you're angry. If you can't control your temper, we can't be together."

3. Seek support: Tonya should confide in someone she trusts, such as a friend or family member. It's important to have a support system and not feel like she's going through this alone.

4. Have an escape plan: Tonya should plan ahead for a safe way to leave the situation if Dan becomes violent or threatening. This could include having a friend on standby to pick her up, or knowing the location of a nearby shelter or safe place.

5. Consider ending the relationship: If Dan continues to exhibit physical red flags despite Tonya's efforts to establish boundaries and seek support, she should seriously consider ending the relationship. No one should have to tolerate physical violence or abuse in a relationship.

## Summary

If you are experiencing physical red flags in your relationship, it's important to seek help immediately. This may involve calling the police, seeking support from a therapist or counselor, and taking steps to protect yourself from further harm. Remember that you have the right to be safe and to live without fear of violence or abuse. Seek help and support from friends, family, and professionals to help you navigate this difficult situation.

## Knowledge Check

Here's an opportunity to assess your understanding and knowledge of the topics we covered in Section B.

### Multiple Choice:

What is a red flag in a relationship?

    a) Something that signals danger or potential harm

    b) Something that is positive and should be celebrated

    c) Something that is irrelevant to the relationship

    d) None of the above

What is an example of a communication red flag?

    a) Active listening

    b) Disrespectful language

    c) Compromise

    d) None of the above

What is an example of a trust red flag?

    a) Being open and honest with your partner

    b) Accusing your partner of cheating without evidence

    c) Giving your partner space and freedom

    d) None of the above

What is an example of an emotional red flag?

    a) Empathy and understanding

    b) Isolating you from friends and family

    c) Being supportive during tough times

    d) None of the above

Which of the following is not an example of a physical red flag?

    a) Refusing to use protection during sex

    b) Using physical force or violence to resolve conflicts

    c) Neglecting personal hygiene

    d) None of the above

What is an example of a financial red flag?

    a) Being open and honest about your financial situation

    b) Controlling your partner's spending habits

    c) Setting financial goals together

    d) None of the above

What is an example of a time red flag?

    a) Both partners prioritize their careers and personal goals

    b) One partner is constantly canceling plans or showing up late

    c) Both partners have different schedules but make an effort to spend quality time together

    d) None of the above

What is an example of a compatibility red flag?

    a) Sharing similar values and beliefs

    b) Having different hobbies or interests

    c) Both partners respect each other's boundaries

    d) None of the above

What is an example of a family red flag?

    a) Having healthy relationships with each other's families

    b) One partner constantly belittles or disrespects the other's family

    c) Both partners come from different cultural backgrounds but respect each other's traditions

    d) None of the above

What should you do if you notice a red flag in your relationship?

    a) Ignore it and hope it goes away on its own

    b) Address it with your partner and have an open and honest conversation

    c) Blame your partner for the red flag and walk away

    d) None of the above

**Knowledge Check**

Here is an opportunity to test your understanding with a true or false examination. Please read each statement carefully and indicate whether it is true or false by selecting the appropriate answer.

1.  Communication red flags are limited to verbal abuse.

2.  All trust red flags are caused by dishonesty.

3.  Emotional red flags are always easy to recognize.

4.  Physical red flags are always visible.

5.  Communication red flags can lead to misunderstandings and conflicts.

6.  Trust red flags can cause emotional stress and anxiety.

7.  Emotional red flags can negatively impact mental health.

8.  Physical red flags can result in physical harm or injury.

9.  It is always easy to identify communication red flags.

10. Emotional red flags can be subtle and difficult to recognize at first.

## Listening to Your Instincts

One of the most important lessons in identifying red flags is learning to trust your instincts. Your instincts are a powerful tool that can help you identify potential problems in a relationship before they become serious. Here are some ways to improve your instincts:

- Pay attention to how you feel when you're around your partner. Do you feel safe and respected, or do you feel uneasy and uncomfortable?

- Trust your gut feelings. If something doesn't feel right, it's important to listen to that feeling and take action.

- Keep a journal of your feelings and experiences in the relationship. This can help you identify patterns and warning signs over time.

- Talk to trusted friends and family members about your relationship. They may be able to provide valuable insight and help you see things from a different perspective.

- Educate yourself about healthy relationships and what red flags to look out for. This knowledge can help you make informed decisions and trust your instincts.

# Warning Signs to Look Out For

There are several warning signs that you should be aware of when identifying red flags in a relationship. These may include:

- Verbal abuse, including name-calling, insults, and put-downs.

- Physical abuse, including hitting, pushing, and other forms of violence.

- Emotional abuse, such as manipulating or controlling behavior, gaslighting, and isolation.

- Sexual abuse, such as coercion or pressure to engage in sexual activities you're uncomfortable with.

- Financial abuse, including controlling your access to money and other resources.

It's important to remember that not all abusive behavior is obvious or overt. In some cases, it may be subtle or disguised as love or concern. Pay attention to any behavior that makes you feel uncomfortable or uneasy and trust your instincts.

## Identifying Manipulative and Coercive Behavior

Manipulative and coercive behavior can be difficult to identify, but it's an essential red flag to be aware of. Here are some signs of manipulative or coercive behavior to look out for:

- Guilt-tripping or shaming you into doing something you're not comfortable with.

- Pressuring you to make decisions quickly or without giving you enough information.

- Gaslighting or denying the reality of a situation to make you doubt your own perceptions.

- Using threats or intimidation to get what they want.

- Isolating you from friends or family members to gain control over you.

- Using affection or kindness as a weapon to manipulate or control you.

Manipulative and coercive behavior can be insidious and may take time to recognize. If you suspect that your partner is engaging in this type of behavior, it's important to reach out for help and support. A trained professional or support group can help you identify red flags and develop a plan to stay safe.

## Knowledge Check

*Here is an opportunity to test your understanding with a true or false examination. Please read each statement carefully and indicate whether it is true or false by selecting the appropriate answer.*

*True or False:*

1. Red flags only occur in romantic relationships.

2. It is important to ignore your instincts when it comes to red flags.

3. Trust is not an important aspect of a healthy relationship.

4. Physical red flags can include any kind of physical abuse.

5. Communication red flags only involve verbal communication.

6. Emotional red flags can lead to mental health issues for the person experiencing them.

7. It is important to make excuses for red flags in a relationship.

8. Manipulative and coercive behavior can be difficult to identify.

9. Warning signs can appear early on in a relationship.

10. Red flags should always be taken seriously and addressed in a relationship.

# Setting Healthy Boundaries

Setting healthy boundaries is essential in any relationship. Boundaries are the limits you set to protect your physical, emotional, and mental health. When someone crosses those boundaries, it can lead to resentment, frustration, and other negative emotions. Examples of healthy boundaries include saying no to requests that make you uncomfortable, speaking up when someone speaks disrespectfully to you, and setting limits on the amount of time you spend with someone. Here are some tips for setting healthy boundaries:

- Identify your boundaries and communicate them clearly

- Don't be afraid to say no when your boundaries are being crossed

- Be consistent in enforcing your boundaries

- Recognize when someone is trying to push your boundaries and stand firm

- Surround yourself with people who respect and support your boundaries

# Communicating Effectively

Effective communication is key in any relationship. It can help to prevent misunderstandings, resolve conflicts, and strengthen the bond between two people. Some people find it challenging to communicate their thoughts and feelings effectively. Here are some tips for effective communication:

- Use "I" statements instead of "you" statements

- Be clear and concise in your communication

- Avoid interrupting the other person while they are speaking

- Listen actively to what the other person is saying

- Be open to feedback and willing to compromise

## Ending a Toxic Relationship

Ending a toxic relationship can be a difficult but necessary step to take for your own well-being. A toxic relationship is characterized by one or both partners engaging in harmful behaviors such as emotional, physical, or sexual abuse. Here are some tips for ending a toxic relationship:

- Acknowledge the situation for what it is

- Take responsibility for your own well-being

- Plan for your safety and well-being

- Cut off all contact with your toxic partner

- Seek help and support from trusted friends, family, or a professional counselor

### Summary

Taking action to set healthy boundaries, communicate effectively, and end a toxic relationship can be challenging but ultimately necessary for your own well-being. Remember that you have the power to take control of your life and make decisions that are in your best interest.

## Knowledge Check

*Using information from this lesson, complete the following sentences by filling in the blanks with the appropriate word(s). Please read each sentence carefully and ensure your answer accurately completes the sentence.*

*Fill in the Blank*

1. ______________ is an important part of maintaining healthy boundaries in relationships.

2. ____________ is an example of a communication red flag.

3. ____________ behavior is a warning sign of a potentially abusive partner.

4. ____________ red flags can include hitting, pushing, and other forms of physical violence.

5. It is important to listen to your ____________ when identifying red flags in a relationship.

6. Setting clear ____________ is an important step in establishing healthy boundaries.

7. Gaslighting is a common form of ____________ behavior.

8. A lack of ____________ in a relationship can be a sign of trust red flags.

9. ____________ is a common emotional red flag in relationships.

10. Ending a toxic relationship may require seeking ____________ support.

# Lesson 2

# Researching Partner's History

Dating can be a thrilling and exciting experience. Meeting someone new and getting to know them on a personal level can be a lot of fun. However, it is important to remember that dating also involves risk. Unfortunately, not everyone is who they say they are, and it is not uncommon for people to hide their true intentions or their past from their partners. This is where the importance of investigating a person's background before dating comes into play. Conducting a background check can provide valuable information that can help prevent potential harm and heartbreak. In this section, we will discuss the risks associated with dating without conducting a background check and the importance of investigating a person's background before dating.

## Investigating a Person's Background Before Dating

In today's digital age, meeting someone new has become easier than ever before. With just a few clicks on a dating app, one can connect with people from all over the world. However, the ease of finding a potential partner also comes with potential risks. In this context, it becomes crucial to investigate a person's background before dating to ensure one's safety and wellbeing.

The statistics reveal that the rate of online dating is growing rapidly. According to a report by Statista, over 30% of US adults have used an online dating app or website. However, with the rise of online dating comes the increase of fraudulent activities, including catfishing, and romance scams. The FBI's Internet Crime Complaint Center (IC3) reported that in 2020 alone, there were over 23,000 complaints of romance scams, with the total reported losses exceeding $605 million.

One of the most significant benefits of investigating a person's background before dating is to avoid potential fraud or catfishing. Catfishing is a term used to describe the practice of luring someone into a relationship by means of a fictional online persona. It can be easy for people to create a false identity on social media, dating apps, and other online platforms. With a little bit of creativity, a fraudster can create a seemingly authentic profile and attract unsuspecting individuals. Investigating a person's background before dating can help one identify any red flags and avoid being a victim of fraud.

Checking a person's background can also provide insight into their criminal history. It is crucial to know if someone has a history of violence, domestic abuse, or any other criminal activity before getting involved in a relationship. It is estimated that one in three women worldwide will experience physical or sexual violence in their lifetime. Therefore, it becomes essential to take preventive measures before getting involved in a relationship.

Another crucial aspect of investigating a person's background before dating is to ensure that they are who they claim to be. There are numerous cases where people have been caught lying about their identity, including their age, occupation, and marital status. In some cases, people may even use fake photos to deceive their potential partners. Investigating a person's background can help identify any discrepancies in their profile and confirm their identity.

When it comes to investigations before marriage, there are specific aspects that need to be considered. Pre-marriage investigations can provide a comprehensive understanding of a person's background, including their financial status, employment history, and personal history. These investigations can help one identify if the potential partner has any outstanding debts, legal issues, or any undisclosed marital status.

## Risks of Dating Without Conducting a Background Check

The importance of conducting a background check before dating someone cannot be overstated. While it may seem like an unnecessary step, the risks of not conducting a background check can be significant. Here are five risks that you should consider before dating someone without doing a background check:

1. You could be dating a criminal: One of the primary reasons for conducting a background check is to uncover any criminal history that the person may have. If you skip this step, you could be putting yourself in danger by dating someone who has a violent or dangerous criminal history.

2. You could be catfished: Catfishing is when someone creates a fake persona online in order to deceive others. This can be particularly dangerous if you are planning to meet the person in real life. Without conducting a background check, you may not realize that the person you are talking to is not who they say they are.

3. You could be dating someone who is married: Believe it or not, some people will lie about their marital status in order to start a relationship with someone. Conducting a background check can help you verify that the person is actually single and available to date.

4. You could be dating someone with a history of domestic violence: Domestic violence is a serious issue that affects many people. If you skip the background check, you may not know if the person you are dating has a history of violent behavior towards their partners.

5. You could be dating someone who is deceptive: People can be deceptive, and dating without conducting a background check can leave you vulnerable to deception. This can include lies about their employment, education, or even their relationship status. A background check can help reveal any discrepancies in the information provided by your potential partner.

Valerie and Ronald met each other through a dating app. They exchanged messages and decided to meet in person at a restaurant. Ronald arrived early and waited for Valerie to arrive. After a few minutes, Valerie arrived, and they introduced themselves. Ronald was instantly attracted to Valerie's beautiful smile and charming personality.

They had a lovely dinner and talked about their interests, hobbies, and future aspirations. Ronald found Valerie to be interesting and engaging. Valerie seemed to be perfect for him, and he felt fortunate to have met her.

As the weeks passed, they went out on more dates, and their relationship grew stronger. However, Ronald started noticing some strange behaviors in Valerie. She would often cancel their plans at the last minute without giving any reasons. She was also secretive about her past and refused to share any information about her family and friends.

One day, Ronald decided to conduct a background check on Valerie. He discovered that Valerie had a history of fraud and had been involved in several cases of identity theft. Ronald was shocked and devastated. He realized that he had been dating a con artist who was only interested in his money. Unfortunately, this was several weeks after, Valerie convinced Ronald to lend her a significant amount of cash. Ronald trusted her and gave her the money without question. He realized that he had fallen victim to a fraudster and regretted not conducting a background check before investing his time and money in the relationship.

This scenario highlights the risks of dating or marrying without conducting a background check. It is essential to take the time to verify the information a potential partner provides and protect yourself from potential fraud and deception.

### Summary

Dating or marrying without conducting a background check can expose you to several risks that can harm you emotionally, physically, or financially. It is important to take precautions to protect yourself and your future. By conducting a background check, you can make an informed decision about whether to pursue a relationship with someone and ensure that you are not putting yourself at risk. Remember, your safety is a top priority, and taking steps to protect yourself is always worth the effort.

## Knowledge Check

Here is an opportunity to evaluate your understanding and knowledge of the topics discussed in Section (A) of lesson 2.

1. Which of the following is a common risk of dating without conducting a background check?

    a.    Falling in love too quickly

    b.    Financial bankruptcy

    c.    Emotional heartbreak

    d.    All of the above

2. What is a potential red flag when conducting a background check?

    a.    A clean criminal record

    b.    Inconsistent employment history

    c.    Positive reviews from former partners

    d.    All of the above

3. What is the purpose of conducting a background check before dating?

    a.    To avoid getting ghosted

    b.    To ensure a potential partner is financially stable

    c.    To protect yourself from potential risks

    d.    None of the above

4. Which of the following is an example of catfishing?

    a.    Using old photos on a dating profile

    b.    Pretending to be someone else online

    c.    Lying about age or occupation

    d.    All of the above

5. What should you do if you discover a potential partner has a criminal history?

    a.    Immediately end the relationship

    b.    Investigate further to understand the charges and circumstances

    c.    Give the person a chance and assume they've changed

    d.    None of the above

6. Which of the following is NOT a reason to conduct a background check before dating?

    a.    Ensuring a potential partner is financially stable

    b.    Checking for a history of infidelity

    c.    Protecting yourself from potential harm

    d.    None of the above

7. What is a potential consequence of not conducting a background check before dating?

    a.    Finding out your partner has a dog when you're allergic

    b.    Financial ruin due to overspending

    c.    Falling in love too quickly

    d.    All of the above

8. What is a common form of fraud in online dating?

    a.    Stealing personal information

    b.    Creating fake profiles

    c.    Pretending to be a wealthy individual

    d.    All of the above

9. Why is it important to be cautious when dating someone with a history of domestic violence?

   a.    They may repeat their violent behavior

   b.    They may be financially unstable

   c.    They may have a criminal history

   d.    None of the above

10. What is the best way to protect yourself when dating?

   a.    Conducting a background check before the first date

   b.    Refusing to share any personal information

   c.    Meeting only in public places

   d.    None of the above

*Fill in the Blank Questions:*

Using information from this lesson, complete the following sentences by filling in the blanks with the appropriate word(s). Please read each sentence carefully and ensure your answer accurately completes the sentence."

1. One of the risks of dating without conducting a background check is financial _________.

2. A potential red flag when conducting a background check is inconsistent _________ history.

3. The purpose of conducting a background check before dating is to protect yourself from potential _________.

4. One example of catfishing is lying about age or _________.

5. If a potential partner has a criminal history, it is important to investigate further to understand the charges and _________.

6.  Conducting a background check before dating can help ensure a potential partner is financially _________.

7.  A potential consequence of not conducting a background check before dating is falling in love too _________.

8.  A common form of fraud in online dating is creating fake _________.

9.  It is important to be cautious when dating someone with a history of domestic violence because they may repeat their _________ behavior.

10. The best way to protect yourself when dating is by conducting a background check before the _________ date.

## Statistics on Dating Violence and Assault

Dating violence and assault are serious issues that can have lasting impacts on victims and society as a whole. According to recent statistics, 1 in 3 adolescents in the US experience some form of dating violence, and 1 in 10 high school students report being physically hurt by a dating partner. Additionally, nearly half of all women and men in the US have experienced psychological aggression by an intimate partner in their lifetime. These alarming numbers highlight the need for increased awareness and prevention efforts surrounding dating violence and assault.

Valerie and Ronald's scenario is unfortunately all too common. In this case, Valerie has been arrested for physical battery against Ronald, which can have serious legal consequences. Ronald may be left with physical and emotional scars that could require counseling or other forms of support. Additionally, he may experience post-traumatic stress disorder (PTSD) or other mental health issues as a result of the violence he experienced.

To address this situation, Ronald may need to seek out counseling or therapy to address the emotional and psychological effects of the abuse. Additionally, he may need to seek out legal resources to ensure his safety and to hold Valerie accountable for her actions. It is important to remember that dating violence and assault can happen to anyone, regardless of gender or sexual orientation, and that it is never the victim's fault.

It is crucial that we continue to raise awareness about the prevalence of dating violence and assault and work to prevent these incidents from occurring. This can be done through education and advocacy efforts, as well as by supporting victims and survivors of dating violence and assault. By taking action to address these issues, we can help create a safer and more equitable society for all.

## Types of Offenders

When it comes to dating, everyone wants to find their perfect match. However, not everyone is honest about their past or present behavior. This can lead to dangerous situations for the unsuspecting partner. It is essential to be aware of the types of offenders that may be encountered when dating without conducting a background check.

One of the most dangerous types of offenders is the sexual predator. These individuals often have a history of sexual assault or rape and may use charm and manipulation to gain the trust of their victims. Another type of offender is the fraudster, who may use fake identities or deceive their partners for financial gain. Other types of offenders include those with a history of violence, drug or alcohol abuse, and those who have been convicted of theft or other crimes. It is important to be aware of these risks and take the necessary precautions to protect yourself when entering into a relationship.

To avoid the risks of dating without conducting a background check, it is important to consider the following measures:

1. Conduct a background check before entering into a relationship with someone.

2. Take things slowly and get to know the person before becoming too involved.

3. Trust your instincts and be aware of any red flags or warning signs.

4. Be cautious about sharing personal information or finances with someone you have just met.

5. Avoid meeting in private or isolated locations until you are comfortable with the person.

6. Stay sober and alert during your dates to be able to make rational decisions.

7. Consider using a dating service that screens its members before allowing them to participate.

By taking these precautions and being aware of the risks involved in dating without conducting a background check, you can protect yourself from potential harm and ensure a safer dating experience.

## The Importance of Knowing a Person's Criminal History

Marriage is a significant commitment, and it is essential to know as much as possible about your partner before taking that step. One crucial aspect to consider is their criminal history. Knowing a person's criminal history before getting married can help ensure that you are entering into a safe and secure relationship. A criminal history check can reveal past convictions or charges, including violent crimes, domestic violence, and drug offenses.

If your partner has a criminal history, it is crucial to have an open and honest conversation about it. This conversation can help establish trust and can also help you determine if you are willing and able to move forward in the relationship. It is also essential to consider the potential legal and financial implications of your partner's criminal history. For example, if your partner has a history of financial fraud or theft, it could impact your joint finances or even lead to legal troubles down the line.

To ensure that you have a comprehensive understanding of your partner's criminal history before getting married, consider the following measures:

1. Conduct a background check that includes criminal history records.

2. Discuss the results of the background check with your partner and have an open and honest conversation about their criminal history.

3. Consider seeking professional advice from a therapist or counselor to help navigate any issues that may arise.

4. Take time to get to know your partner and their family and friends to gather more information about their character and past behavior.

5. Consider the severity and nature of the past convictions or charges before making a decision about the relationship.

6. Be aware of any legal or financial implications that may arise as a result of your partner's criminal history.

7. Trust your instincts and be aware of any red flags or warning signs in the relationship.

Making sure you are aware of your partner's criminal history before getting married is imperative to making informed decisions and entering into a safe and secure relationship.

# The Risk of Identity Theft

In recent years, online dating has become increasingly popular, with millions of people using dating apps and websites to meet potential partners. While online dating can be a convenient way to connect with others, it also comes with potential risks, including the risk of identity theft. Identity theft occurs when someone uses another person's personal information, such as their name, date of birth, or social security number, without their knowledge or consent.

Research has shown that online dating platforms are an attractive target for identity thieves. The anonymity of online communication can make it easier for scammers to gain access to personal information, and the ease of setting up fake profiles can make it more difficult to verify the identity of potential dates. In light of these risks, it is essential for individuals to take steps to protect their personal information while dating online.

To address the risk of identity theft while dating online, researchers have recommended the following measures:

1. Be cautious about sharing personal information, such as your full name, date of birth, or social security number.

2. Use secure communication channels, such as encrypted messaging apps, to communicate with potential dates.

3. Be aware of common phishing scams and do not click on links or download attachments from unfamiliar sources.

4. Check your credit report regularly to detect any unauthorized activity.

5. Be cautious of requests for money or financial assistance, as these may be signs of a scam.

6.  Conduct a background check on potential dates to verify their identity.

7.  Report any suspicious activity to the dating platform or law enforcement authorities.

Using these recommendations, individuals can reduce the risk of identity theft and protect their personal information when dating online. With online dating continuing to gain popularity, it is imperative for individuals to remain vigilant and take precautions to protect their personal information.

**Knowledge Check**

Here is an opportunity to evaluate your understanding and knowledge of the topics discussed in Section (B) if lesson 2.

*True or False*

1.  Identity theft is a common risk associated with online dating.

2.  Sharing personal information with someone you barely know can increase the risk of identity theft.

3.  Conducting a background check on a potential date is not an effective way to reduce the risk of identity theft.

4.  Using secure messaging apps to communicate with a potential date can help protect your personal information.

5.  Phishing scams are not a common risk associated with online dating.

6.  Checking your credit report regularly can help you detect any unauthorized activity related to identity theft.

7.  Requests for money or financial assistance from a potential date are usually not signs of a scam.

8.  The anonymity of online communication makes it easier for identity thieves to gain access to personal information.

9.  The risks of identity theft are the same for online dating and traditional dating.

10. Reporting suspicious activity to the dating platform or law enforcement authorities can help prevent identity theft.

Lesson

# 3

# BACKGROUND CHECK 101

# Methods of Conducting a Background Check

Background checks are an essential part of many industries, including human resources, security, and law enforcement. There are several methods of conducting a background check, each with its own strengths and limitations. One of the most common methods is to use an online background check service, which can provide a range of information, including criminal records, employment history, and credit reports. However, online background checks are not always comprehensive or up-to-date, and may miss important information.

Another method of conducting a background check is to contact the relevant authorities directly, such as the police department or county clerk's office, to request public records. This method can provide more accurate and up to date information but may be more time-consuming and require more effort. Additionally, not all public records are available to the public, and some may require a court order to access. Other methods of conducting a background check include contacting references and conducting social media searches.

When conducting a background check, it is important to consider the purpose of the check and to use multiple methods to ensure accuracy and completeness. Some tips for conducting a background check include:

1. Identify the purpose of the check and the information that is relevant.

2. Obtain written consent from the individual being checked.

3. Use multiple methods to ensure accuracy and completeness.

4. Verify the accuracy of the information obtained.

5. Consider the context of the information obtained and avoid making judgments based on incomplete or misleading information.

6. Be aware of legal requirements and privacy considerations.

7. Use the information obtained to make informed decisions while respecting the individual's rights and privacy.

## What to Look for in a Background Check

Getting to know your partner well is essential when considering a serious relationship or marriage. Investigating their past is one way to gain valuable insight. The results of a background check can provide you with valuable information about your partner's criminal record, financial history, and personal behavior. You can make an informed decision about your future together by conducting a thorough background check.

Here are seven essential items to look for in a background check when considering a serious relationship:

1. Identity verification, including name, date of birth, and social security number: This information is critical for verifying your partner's identity and ensuring that they are who they claim to be.

2. Employment history, including job titles and responsibilities: This information can help you better understand your partner's career path and work habits.

3. Education history, including degrees earned and institutions attended: This information can help you better understand your partner's intellectual interests and educational background.

4. Criminal record, including any misdemeanors or felonies: This information can provide insight into your partner's past behavior and any potential risks.

5. Credit history, including any bankruptcies or defaults: This information can help you better understand your partner's financial history and their ability to manage money.

6. Personal references, which can help verify your partner's character and work history: This information can provide additional insights into your partner's personality and behavior.

7. Licenses and certifications, which can confirm any specialized skills or training: This information can help you better understand your partner's abilities and potential career opportunities.

Knowing the details of your partner's past is a necessary step to understanding the stability and commitment of your relationship. A background check can reveal so much about your partner's character, so it's an important part of the process of deciding whether or not to take the relationship to the next level.

Let's imagine that Bill and Tyra have been dating for a year and are thinking about getting married. Before making a lifelong commitment, they decide to conduct a background check. Bill has a stable job, a clean criminal record, and a good credit history. Tyra has a master's degree, a stable job, and a clean criminal record, but she has a significant amount of credit card debt. After reviewing the results of their background checks, they discuss their findings and decide to work together to manage Tyra's debt. By conducting a background check, they were able to make an informed decision about their future together and take steps to build a strong foundation for their relationship.

A background check can be an essential tool for anyone considering a serious relationship or marriage. By conducting a thorough background check, you can gain valuable insights into your partner's past behavior and financial history. While a background check should not be used to pass judgment on your partner, it can provide a valuable context for making an informed decision about your future together. Ultimately, the decision to conduct a background check is a personal one and should be based on your own needs and concerns. Making an informed decision about your future together can lead to a stronger, more fulfilling relationship when you conduct a background check.

# How to Interpret the Results of a Background Check

When investigating a potential spouse for a relationship, conducting a background check can provide valuable insights into their past behavior and history. However, interpreting the results of a background check can be a daunting task, and it's essential to know what to look for and how to interpret the information you receive. By understanding the following seven key items, you can make informed decisions about your potential partner's past and whether they are a good fit for a relationship:

1. Criminal history: A criminal record can reveal potential red flags and risk factors that could impact your relationship.

2. Financial history: A person's financial history can be a significant factor in a relationship, and it's essential to understand their credit score, outstanding debts, and bankruptcy history.

3. Employment history: A person's employment history can reveal their work ethic, career goals, and level of commitment to their job.

4. Education history: Education history can provide insight into a person's intellectual curiosity, career aspirations, and level of dedication to personal growth.

5. Social media presence: A person's social media presence can reveal a lot about their personality, interests, and social habits, and it's essential to consider how this could impact your relationship.

6. Family background: Understanding a person's family history and relationships with family members can help you understand their values, beliefs, and how they approach family relationships.

7. Previous relationships: Learning about a person's previous relationships can provide valuable insights into their emotional maturity, communication style, and how they handle conflict.

Now, let's consider a scenario in which Bill and Tyra are considering a serious relationship. Bill has asked Tyra to marry him, and she is considering his proposal. Before making a decision, Tyra decides to conduct a background check on Bill to learn more about his past. She hires a reputable background check company and receives a report containing information about Bill's criminal history, financial history, employment history, education history, social media presence, family background, and previous relationships.

After reviewing the report, Tyra notices that Bill has a history of bankruptcy and outstanding debts, which raises concerns about his financial stability. Additionally, the report reveals that Bill has a criminal record, including a DUI conviction from several years ago. While Bill has been open and honest about his past, Tyra is concerned about how these issues could impact their future together.

Tyra decides to have a conversation with Bill about her concerns and how they can work together to address these challenges. Through open communication and a willingness to work together, they are able to overcome these obstacles and build a strong foundation for their future together. In this scenario, the background check served as a valuable tool for Tyra to make an informed decision about her potential spouse, and ultimately, it helped them to build a stronger relationship based on honesty and trust.

But in the case of Franklin and Diana, after receiving the background check report on Diana, Franklin was shocked and disappointed. He had hoped that she would have been forthcoming about her past, but it seemed that there were some significant details that she had omitted. The report showed that Diana had been arrested twice in the past for driving under the influence of alcohol and had a history of multiple traffic violations. Additionally, the report revealed that Diana had filed for bankruptcy several years ago and had not been able to pay off all of his debts.

Franklin realized that these issues were significant red flags and could have serious implications for their future together. He was especially concerned about the DUI arrests, as it suggested that Diana had a drinking problem that she had not disclosed to him. Franklin knew that he could not ignore these problems and decided that it was best for him to end the relationship before it went any further.

Although it was a difficult decision, Franklin knew that he had made the right choice for himself. He did not want to be in a relationship with someone who was not honest and transparent with her about their past and current situation. While it was disappointing to end things with Diana, Franklin knew that it was better to end the relationship now rather than to continue with someone who had potential deal-breaking issues in their background.

Again, knowing the details of your partner's past is a necessary step to understanding the stability and commitment of your relationship. Background checks reveal a lot about your partner, so they're an important part of the process of deciding whether or not to continue a relationship.

## How to Have a Conversation About Background Checks with Potential Partners

When it comes to investigating potential partners for a relationship, conducting a background check can be an important step to take. However, it can also be a sensitive and potentially awkward topic to broach with a new partner. Having a conversation about background checks can help to establish trust and transparency in a relationship. Here are some tips on how to have a conversation about background checks with potential partners:

1. Start the conversation early: It's important to bring up the topic of background checks early in a relationship, before things become too serious. This will help to avoid any surprises or misunderstandings down the line.

2. Be honest about your intentions: When bringing up the topic of background checks, it's important to be clear about why you're interested in conducting one. Let your potential partner know that you value transparency and honesty in a relationship and that you want to make sure you're both on the same page.

3. Be respectful: When asking someone about their background, it's important to be respectful and non-judgmental. Remember that everyone has a past and that you're not trying to pass judgment, but rather to gain a better understanding of who they are.

4. Be open to sharing: If you're asking your potential partner about their background, be prepared to share information about your own as well. This will help to establish trust and show that you're not just trying to pry into their personal life.

5. Discuss the types of information you're looking for: Before conducting a background check, it's important to discuss the types of information that you're interested in. This will help to ensure that both parties are on the same page and that there are no misunderstandings.

6. Be prepared to answer questions: If your potential partner has questions about the background check process or why you're interested in conducting one, be prepared to answer them honestly and openly.

7. Respect their decision: While it's important to have a conversation about background checks, it's also important to respect your potential partner's decision if they're not comfortable with the idea. If they decline to participate in a background check, it's important to accept their decision and move forward.

Having a conversation about background checks with potential partners can be a sensitive topic, but it's an important step in establishing trust and transparency in a relationship. By following these tips, you can help to ensure that the conversation is respectful, honest, and productive.

As an example, scenario, let's consider a situation where Sarah and Alex have been dating for a few months, and Sarah is interested in conducting a background check on Alex. Here's how Sarah might approach the conversation:

Sarah: "Hey Alex, I wanted to talk to you about something that's been on my mind. I hope you don't mind me bringing it up." Alex: "Sure, what's on your mind?"

Sarah: "Well, I was thinking about conducting a background check on you. I know it might seem like a sensitive topic, but I think it's important for us to be transparent with each other about our pasts." Alex: "Uh, I don't know how I feel about that. Why do you want to conduct a background check?"

Sarah: "I want to make sure that we're both on the same page and that there are no surprises down the line. I think it's important to establish trust and transparency in our relationship, and conducting a background check can help with that." Alex: "I don't know. It feels a little invasive."

Sarah: "I understand that it can feel that way. But I want to be clear that I'm not trying to pass judgment on you or pry into your personal life. I just want to make sure we're both being honest and open with each other."

Alex: "Okay, I see where you're coming from. I suppose I don't have anything to hide, so I'm willing to go through with it. But can we talk about what kind of information you're looking for and how you're planning to conduct the check?"

Sarah: "Of course, I understand that this can be a sensitive topic. I'm planning on using a reputable online service that conducts thorough background checks, but we can also discuss any specific concerns or questions you may have about the process."

Alex: "Alright, that sounds reasonable. Just to be clear, are you planning on sharing the results of the background check with me?"

Sarah: "Absolutely. I think it's important that we both have access to the information and that we can discuss it together. It's not about pointing fingers or assigning blame, but rather about building trust and ensuring that we have a healthy and honest relationship."

Alex: "Okay, I understand. Let's go ahead with it and see what we find."

Sarah: "Thank you for being willing to have this conversation with me. I think it shows that we're both committed to building a strong and transparent relationship."

It is important to note that having a discussion about background checks with a potential partner may seem intrusive or uncomfortable, but it is an important step in establishing trust and transparency in a relationship. When both partners discuss the reasons for conducting a background check and treat the topic with sensitivity and respect, they will feel more secure in their relationship and avoid unpleasant surprises in the future. Consider approaching the topic open-mindedly and listening to your partner's concerns, and the conversation can lead to a stronger and more honest relationship.

**Summary**

As we close this lesson on methods of conducting a background check for potential partners, it's important to remember that while these checks can be helpful, they are not foolproof. The information provided through a background check should be used as a tool in conjunction with open and honest communication with your potential partner.

When conducting a background check, it's important to use reputable sources and to consider the limitations of the information provided. In addition, it's important to be aware of what to look for in a background check, including criminal history, employment history, and financial history.

Interpreting the results of a background check can be a nuanced process, and it's important to consider the context of any information found. It's also important to have open and honest conversations with your potential partner about the information found, and to approach the conversation in a respectful and non-judgmental manner.

Finally, if you do decide to have a conversation about conducting a background check with a potential partner, it's important to approach the conversation in a respectful and transparent manner. Clearly communicate your intentions and the reasons for wanting to conduct a background check and be open to discussing any concerns or questions your partner may have. Remember, the goal of conducting a background check is to establish trust and transparency in a relationship, not to pass judgment or invade privacy.

## Knowledge Check

Here is an opportunity.." to Here is an opportunity to test your understanding of Lesson 3 with a true or false examination on Section (A). Please read each statement carefully and indicate whether it is true or false by selecting the appropriate answer.

1. A background check can reveal criminal records.

2. Credit history is not important to consider in a background check.

3. It is legal to perform a background check on someone without their consent.

4. Social media profiles cannot be used to gather information for a background check.

5. Employment history is not relevant to a background check.

6. A background check can reveal if someone is married or has children.

7. It is not necessary to perform a background check if you already know the person well.

8.  A background check can provide information on someone's education history.

9.  A background check is a foolproof way to ensure a potential partner is trustworthy.

10. A background check can reveal if someone has a history of substance abuse.

11. Driving records are not included in a standard background check.

12. You cannot perform a background check on someone who lives in another country.

13. A background check can reveal if someone has ever filed for bankruptcy.

14. Social Security numbers are not needed to perform a background check.

15. A background check can reveal if someone has a history of domestic violence.

16. A background check can provide information on someone's immigration status.

17. It is unethical to perform a background check on someone without their knowledge.

18. A background check can reveal if someone has a history of mental health issues.

19. A background check can provide information on someone's property ownership.

20. It is impossible to perform a background check on someone who has never had a job.

# Lesson

# 4

# Love and Credit Scores

# The Importance of Good Credit in Committed Relationships

Financial stability plays an important role in determining a person's potential as a romantic partner today. Good credit is one aspect of financial stability that is often overlooked. Having good credit is an indicator of financial responsibility and can have a significant impact on a couple's ability to obtain loans, mortgages, and other financial assets together. When entering into a committed relationship, it is important to take into account a potential partner's credit score and financial history.

A good credit score indicates that the individual is responsible with money and is able to make timely payments. A person's ability to manage money in a relationship can be an indicator of his or her overall financial health. Poor credit scores, however, may be indicative of future financial difficulties. Suppose a couple wishes to purchase a home or a car together but has a poor credit score. This could make it more difficult to secure a loan or result in higher interest rates, ultimately costing them more money.

In addition to the practical benefits of good credit, such as the ability to secure loans and mortgages, there are also emotional and psychological benefits to being financially responsible. Being financially stable can reduce stress and anxiety in a relationship, which can have a positive impact on a couple's overall well-being. Additionally, being able to manage money effectively can help couples achieve their shared goals and aspirations, such as traveling, starting a family, or saving for retirement. By working together to build good credit and maintain financial stability, couples can strengthen their relationship and build a solid foundation for their future together.

However, it's important to note that having good credit should not be the sole determining factor in a relationship. While financial stability is important, it should not overshadow other important aspects of a healthy relationship, such as mutual respect, communication, and trust. It's crucial to approach financial discussions with sensitivity and understanding, as money can be a sensitive topic for many people.

# Link between credit scores and committed relationships

In recent years, research has suggested that credit scores may play a significant role in determining the success of committed relationships. While credit scores are primarily used to assess a person's financial responsibility, they can also be used as a proxy for other important relationship factors, such as trustworthiness, dependability, and future stability. Thus, it is becoming increasingly important for individuals to consider their own credit score and that of their potential partner when entering into a committed relationship.

Studies have found that there is a correlation between credit scores and the likelihood of divorce. A study conducted by the Federal Reserve Board found that couples with similar credit scores were more likely to stay together than those with dissimilar credit scores. Similarly, a study by the Brookings Institution found that credit scores can be used as a predictor of the likelihood of divorce. The study found that a couple's average credit score at the beginning of their relationship was a strong predictor of their likelihood of divorce in the future.

One possible explanation for the link between credit scores and committed relationships is that credit scores can be a proxy for other important relationship factors, such as trustworthiness and dependability. A person with a high credit score may be perceived as more trustworthy and responsible, while a person with a low credit score may be perceived as less reliable and less likely to follow through on commitments. Additionally, credit scores may reflect a person's future stability and potential to contribute to a long-term relationship. A person with a good credit score may have a stable job and financial outlook, which can contribute to a stable and healthy relationship.

It's important to note, however, that credit scores should not be the only factor considered when entering into a committed relationship. While financial stability is important, it should not overshadow other important aspects of a healthy relationship, such as mutual respect, communication, and trust. Additionally, credit scores are not always an accurate reflection of a person's financial situation, as there are many factors that can impact a credit score. Thus, it's important to approach financial discussions with sensitivity and understanding, and to view credit scores as just one piece of a larger puzzle when assessing the potential success of a committed relationship.

The link between credit scores and committed relationships has become an increasingly important topic in recent years. While credit scores are primarily used to assess a person's financial responsibility, they can also be used as a proxy for other important relationship factors, such as trustworthiness, dependability, and future stability. As a result, it is becoming more common for individuals to consider their own credit score and that of their potential partner when entering into a committed relationship.

Several studies have found a correlation between credit scores and the likelihood of divorce. For example, a study conducted by the Federal Reserve Board found that couples with similar credit scores were more likely to stay together than those with dissimilar credit scores. Similarly, a study by the Brookings Institution found that a couple's average credit score at the beginning of their relationship was a strong predictor of their likelihood of divorce in the future. These findings suggest that credit scores may play a significant role in the success of committed relationships.

One possible explanation for the link between credit scores and committed relationships is that credit scores can be a proxy for other important relationship factors. For example, a person with a high credit score may be perceived as more trustworthy and responsible, while a person with a low credit score may be perceived as less reliable and less likely to follow through on commitments. Additionally, credit scores may reflect a person's future stability and potential to contribute to a long-term relationship. A person with a good credit score may have a stable job and financial outlook, which can contribute to a stable and healthy relationship.

However, it's important to note that credit scores should not be the only factor considered when entering into a committed relationship. While financial stability is important, it should not overshadow other important aspects of a healthy relationship, such as mutual respect, communication, and trust. Additionally, credit scores are not always an accurate reflection of a person's financial situation, as there are many factors that can impact a credit score.

For example, a person may have a low credit score due to circumstances outside of their control, such as a medical emergency or a job loss. In these cases, it may be unfair to judge the person solely based on their credit score. Furthermore, it's important to approach financial discussions with sensitivity and understanding, as discussing finances can be a sensitive topic for many individuals.

When considering the link between credit scores and committed relationships, it's also important to consider the impact that financial stress can have on a relationship. Financial stress can cause tension and disagreements between partners and can ultimately lead to the breakdown of the relationship. By being open and transparent about their financial situation and working together to develop a financial plan, couples can avoid unnecessary stress and build a stronger, more resilient relationship.

It's also important to recognize that credit scores can be improved over time with the right financial habits and strategies. By paying bills on time, keeping credit card balances low, and checking their credit report regularly, individuals can improve their credit score and build a more stable financial future for themselves and their potential partner.

In conclusion, while credit scores can be a useful tool in assessing the potential success of a committed relationship, they should not be the only factor considered. Trust, communication, and mutual respect are all crucial components of a healthy relationship and should be given equal weight when evaluating a potential partner. By working together to develop a strong financial plan and being open and transparent about their financial situation, couples can build a more stable and fulfilling relationship, regardless of their individual credit scores.

## How Poor Credit Can Negatively Affect a Relationship

Financial matters can often cause tension and stress in any relationship, and poor credit is no exception. Poor credit scores can negatively impact a couple's financial future and even their personal lives. This academic content aims to explore how poor credit can negatively affect a relationship and what steps can be taken to mitigate these effects.

Poor credit can strain a relationship by limiting the couple's access to financial resources, making it difficult to secure loans, credit cards, or even basic necessities like a rental apartment. If one partner has a poor credit score, it can make it challenging for the couple to access joint credit accounts or take out a loan together. Additionally, if the partner with a poor credit score is unable to pay their bills, their credit score may continue to deteriorate, causing a ripple effect that can negatively impact the couple's joint financial health. Poor credit scores can also lead to higher interest rates on loans or credit cards, increasing the couple's debt burden and making it harder for them to achieve financial stability.

Poor credit can also have an emotional toll on a relationship. It can cause stress and anxiety, leading to arguments and disagreements about money. When one partner has a poor credit score, the other partner may feel like they are shouldering the financial burden of the relationship, leading to feelings of resentment and frustration. In extreme cases, poor credit scores can lead to separation or divorce. Financial stress is one of the leading causes of divorce, and poor credit scores can exacerbate the problem. Therefore, it is essential for couples to have open and honest conversations about their finances and work together to improve their credit scores.

Poor credit can impact a couple's ability to plan for the future. For example, a low credit score can make it difficult to secure a mortgage, making it harder for the couple to purchase a home or investment property. This can limit their options for building long-term wealth and can put a strain on their personal and financial goals. Poor credit can also limit a couple's ability to plan for other major expenses like starting a family, pursuing higher education, or investing in a business. These limitations can create stress and uncertainty in the relationship, further straining the couple's emotional connection.

It is crucial for couples to understand how poor credit can negatively impact their relationship and take steps to mitigate its effects. One way to improve credit scores is by paying bills on time and reducing debt. Couples can work together to create a budget and develop a debt repayment plan. Additionally, couples can consult with financial advisors or credit counselors to create a plan for improving their credit scores. By taking proactive steps to improve their financial health, couples can reduce the strain that poor credit can put on their relationship and work towards a brighter financial future together.

# Benefits of having good credit in a committed relationship

Financial stability is a crucial component of any healthy relationship, and credit scores play a significant role in achieving this stability. Good credit scores can positively impact a couple's financial future and even their personal lives. This academic content aims to explore how good credit can positively affect a relationship and what steps couples can take to maintain and improve their credit scores.

Good credit scores can provide a couple with more financial options and opportunities. It can make it easier for the couple to secure loans or credit cards with favorable interest rates, allowing them to access joint credit accounts or take out a loan together. This financial flexibility can also help the couple achieve their personal and shared goals, such as purchasing a home, starting a business, or pursuing higher education. Good credit scores can also make it easier for the couple to secure rental apartments or other necessary housing arrangements, ensuring a stable and secure living situation.

Good credit scores can also positively impact a couple's emotional well-being. Financial stress is a common cause of relationship strain and can lead to arguments and disagreements about money. When a couple has good credit scores, they can reduce financial stress, leading to a more peaceful and harmonious relationship. Additionally, good credit scores can instill a sense of financial responsibility and independence in both partners, leading to increased trust and respect in the relationship. When both partners take an active role in maintaining good credit scores, it can create a sense of teamwork and collaboration, strengthening the bond between them.

Good credit scores can positively impact a couple's long-term financial future. A high credit score can make it easier for the couple to secure loans or credit cards with favorable interest rates, reducing their debt burden and making it easier for them to achieve financial stability. Additionally, good credit scores can make it easier for the couple to plan for the future, such as saving for retirement or planning for unexpected expenses. Good credit scores can also provide a couple with more investment opportunities, allowing them to build wealth and create a stable financial foundation for their future.

Maintaining good credit scores requires active and ongoing effort from both partners. Couples can work together to create a budget, track their expenses, and make timely payments on bills and debts. Additionally, couples can monitor their credit reports regularly and dispute any errors or inaccuracies. Good credit scores can also be achieved by keeping credit card balances low and avoiding excessive debt. By taking proactive steps to maintain good credit scores, couples can ensure a strong and stable financial foundation for their relationship and future together.

Financial stability is a crucial component of any healthy relationship, and credit scores play a significant role in achieving this stability. Good credit scores can provide a couple with more financial options and opportunities, positively impacting their long-term financial future and even their personal lives. Maintaining good credit scores requires active and ongoing effort from both partners. By taking proactive steps to maintain and improve their credit scores, couples can ensure a strong and stable financial foundation for their relationship and future together.

Good credit scores can make it easier for a couple to secure loans or credit cards with favorable interest rates, allowing them to access joint credit accounts or take out a loan together. This financial flexibility can help the couple achieve their personal and shared goals, such as purchasing a home, starting a business, or pursuing higher education. Good credit scores can also make it easier for the couple to secure rental apartments or other necessary housing arrangements, ensuring a stable and secure living situation. Additionally, a high credit score can make it easier for the couple to plan for the future, such as saving for retirement or planning for unexpected expenses. Good credit scores can provide a couple with more investment opportunities, allowing them to build wealth and create a stable financial foundation for their future. With good credit scores, a couple can access better investment opportunities such as stocks, bonds, and mutual funds, which can help them build a diverse portfolio and increase their net worth over time.

Good credit scores can also positively impact a couple's emotional well-being. Financial stress is a common cause of relationship strain and can lead to arguments and disagreements about money. When a couple has good credit scores, they can reduce financial stress, leading to a more peaceful and harmonious relationship. Additionally, good credit scores can instill a sense of financial responsibility and independence in both partners, leading to increased trust and respect in the relationship. When both partners take an active role in maintaining good credit scores, it can create a sense of teamwork and collaboration, strengthening the bond between them.

Maintaining good credit scores requires ongoing effort from both partners. Couples can work together to create a budget, track their expenses, and make timely payments on bills and debts. Regularly monitoring credit reports and disputing any errors or inaccuracies can also help maintain good credit scores. Couples can also keep credit card balances low and avoid excessive debt by paying off credit card balances in full each month and avoiding unnecessary spending.

Couples can also take steps to improve their credit scores if they have less than ideal credit. One way to do this is by paying off debt and making timely payments on bills and credit accounts. It is also important to keep credit card balances low and avoid opening too many credit accounts at once. Couples can also consider seeking the advice of a financial advisor or credit counselor who can help them develop a plan to improve their credit scores.

## Summary

Good credit scores can positively impact a couple's financial future and personal lives, providing them with more financial options and reducing financial stress in their relationship. Maintaining good credit scores requires ongoing effort from both partners, but the benefits are worth it. Couples who work together to maintain and improve their credit scores can create a strong and stable financial foundation for their relationship and future together. With good credit scores, a couple can achieve their personal and shared financial goals and build a brighter future together.

## Knowledge Check

Knowledge Check: Here is an opportunity to test your understanding with a true or false examination. Please read each statement carefully and indicate whether it is true or false by selecting the appropriate answer.

1. Good credit scores can provide a couple with more financial options.

2. Good credit scores can reduce financial stress in a marriage.

3. Good credit scores can lead to a more harmonious relationship.

4. Good credit scores can lead to increased trust and respect in a marriage.

5. Couples with good credit scores have access to better investment opportunities.

6. Good credit scores can help a couple build wealth over time.

7. Regularly monitoring credit reports is not necessary to maintain good credit scores.

8. Paying off credit card balances in full each month can help maintain good credit scores.

9. Good credit scores can help a couple achieve their financial goals.

10. Good credit scores are not important in a marriage relationship.

# TALKING FOR

# LASTING LOVE

Communication is the foundation of any successful relationship, and this is especially true in marriage. While many couples start their journey with open and honest communication, it's not uncommon for communication to break down over time. Whether due to stress, miscommunication, or simply growing apart, the loss of effective communication can put a serious strain on a marriage. In this article, we'll explore the importance of effective communication in marital relationships, provide examples of how communication can break down, and offer practical tips and strategies for improving communication with your partner.

*Statistics:*

The importance of effective communication in marriage is backed by numerous studies. Here are just a few statistics that highlight its significance:

- According to a study by the University of Denver, couples who reported high levels of communication and satisfaction in their relationship were less likely to divorce than those who reported low levels of communication and satisfaction.

- A survey by the Gottman Institute found that the most successful couples communicate their feelings and needs clearly and make an effort to understand their partner's perspective.

- In a survey by the American Association for Marriage and Family Therapy, 93% of respondents said that improving communication was the most important step couples can take to resolve their problems.

*Examples:*

Let's take a look at a couple of examples to illustrate how communication breakdowns can impact a marriage:

- John and Sarah have been married for 10 years. They used to communicate regularly and openly, but over the years, they've grown apart. They've become less interested in each other's lives and haven't been able to have deep conversations about their thoughts and feelings. They've also started to keep secrets from each other, which has caused a further breakdown in communication. Now, John and Sarah feel like they're living separate lives and are struggling to reconnect.

- Mike and Karen have been married for 5 years. They used to communicate effectively, but over time, they've started to argue more and listen less. When they argue, they both tend to raise their voices and interrupt each other. This has led to a cycle of frustration and defensiveness, and they're finding it harder to resolve conflicts. Karen has started to withdraw from conversations altogether, which has only made things worse.

*Tips for Effective Communication:*

If you're looking to improve your communication with your partner, here are some tips to get you started:

1. Practice Active Listening: When your partner is speaking, give them your full attention. Put away distractions like your phone or laptop and avoid interrupting them. When they're finished speaking, take a moment to reflect on what they said and respond thoughtfully.

2. Use "I" Statements: Instead of saying "you did this" or "you made me feel this way," use "I" statements to express how you feel. For example, "I felt hurt when you didn't show up to our dinner plans," is more effective than "You always ditch me."

3. Avoid Criticism and Defensiveness: Criticism and defensiveness can quickly derail a conversation. Instead of attacking your partner or becoming defensive, try to express your needs and feelings in a non-judgmental way. For example, instead of saying "You never help out around the house," try saying "I feel overwhelmed with the housework, and I could really use your help."

4. Take Breaks When Needed: If you feel overwhelmed or frustrated during a conversation, take a break and come back to it later. This can help you both cool off and approach the conversation with a fresh perspective.

5. Express Appreciation and Gratitude: Make an effort to express appreciation and gratitude for your partner regularly, even for small things. This can help build a positive atmosphere in your relationship and make it easier to communicate when conflicts arise.

6. Be Respectful: Respect is key in any relationship. Make sure to listen to your partner's opinions and validate their feelings, even if you disagree. Avoid name-calling, insults, and other disrespectful behaviors.

7. Use Humor: Humor can be a great way to diffuse tension and lighten the mood. However, make sure to use it appropriately and avoid using sarcasm or humor as a way to criticize or belittle your partner.

8. Practice Empathy: Empathy means putting yourself in your partner's shoes and trying to understand their perspective. This can help you better communicate with each other and find solutions that work for both of you.

9. Schedule Time to Talk: Life can get busy, and it's easy for communication to fall by the wayside. Make an effort to schedule regular time to talk with your partner, whether it's a weekly date night or a daily check-in.

10. Seek Help When Needed: If you're struggling with communication in your marriage, don't be afraid to seek help. Couples therapy can be a great way to learn new communication skills and work through conflicts in a safe and supportive environment.

## Summary

Effective communication is essential for a healthy and happy marriage. By practicing active listening, using "I" statements, avoiding criticism and defensiveness, taking breaks when needed, expressing appreciation and gratitude, being respectful, using humor appropriately, practicing empathy, scheduling time to talk, and seeking help when needed, you can improve your communication with your partner and build a stronger, more fulfilling relationship. Remember, communication takes effort and practice, but the rewards are well worth it.

## Knowledge Check

Using information from this lesson, complete the following sentences by filling in the blanks with the appropriate word(s). Please read each sentence carefully and ensure your answer accurately completes the sentence.

1. _________ is key in any relationship.

2. Active _________ is an important component of effective communication.

3. Using "I" statements instead of _________ can help reduce defensiveness.

4. When conflicts arise, taking a _________ can help you both calm down and think more clearly.

5. Expressing _________ and gratitude can help maintain a positive atmosphere in your relationship.

6. Avoiding _________ and insults is essential for respectful communication.

7. Humor can be a great way to _________ tension and lighten the mood.

8. Practicing _________ means putting yourself in your partner's shoes and trying to understand their perspective.

9.  Life can get busy, so it's important to _________ regular time to talk with your partner.

10. Couples therapy can be a great way to learn new communication skills and work through conflicts in a safe and supportive _________.

11. When communicating with your partner, try to avoid using the words "always" or "_________."

12. Making eye contact and using _________ language can help convey sincerity and trustworthiness.

13. _________ listening involves paying attention to what your partner is saying and responding appropriately.

14. When discussing sensitive topics, it's important to _________ your partner's feelings and opinions.

15. It's important to _________ your partner's point of view, even if you don't agree with it.

16. _________ feedback is a helpful tool for improving communication and resolving conflicts.

17. When communicating with your partner, try to stay focused on the _________ at hand.

18. Using _________ phrases like "I understand how you feel" can help validate your partner's emotions.

19. When you're feeling angry or upset, it can be helpful to take a _________ before responding to your partner.

20. When seeking help for communication issues, it's important to find a therapist who specializes in _________ therapy.

# Lesson

# 6

# Building For Deeper Connections

Romantic relationships are complex and multifaceted, involving a range of emotions, expectations, and challenges. One essential aspect of building and maintaining a healthy, satisfying relationship is effective communication, which can be facilitated by the art of questioning. Asking questions can foster connection, deepen understanding, and enhance intimacy. However, not all questions are created equal, and the way in which questions are asked can greatly impact their effectiveness. In this article, we will explore the art of questioning in romantic relationships, providing examples and tips for enhancing connection, communication, and understanding.

## The Power of Questions in Romantic Relationships

Questions have the power to unlock meaningful conversations, facilitate self-awareness, and deepen intimacy. When we ask questions in a relationship, we demonstrate our interest and curiosity in our partner's thoughts, feelings, and experiences. This, in turn, can create a sense of emotional safety and trust, leading to greater openness and vulnerability. By asking questions, we also gain valuable insights into our partner's perspective, which can enhance empathy and understanding.

*Examples:*

- "How are you feeling about our relationship right now?"

- "What is one thing that you appreciate about me?"

- "What was your experience like growing up?"

Types of Questions to Ask (and Avoid) in Romantic Relationships

Not all questions are created equal, and some types of questions can be more effective than others in facilitating connection, communication, and understanding. Below are some examples of types of questions that can be helpful (and some to avoid) in romantic relationships.

Open-Ended Questions: Open-ended questions invite more than a yes or no answer, and encourage your partner to share more details and feelings. They can be especially helpful for exploring complex or sensitive topics.

*Examples:*

- "How do you feel about our future together?"

- "What is your biggest fear in our relationship?"

- "What do you need from me right now?"

Avoid: Closed-Ended Questions: Closed-ended questions are questions that can be answered with a simple "yes" or "no" or a short response. These types of questions do not encourage in-depth conversation or facilitate understanding.

*Examples:*

- "Do you love me?"

- "Are you happy in our relationship?"

- "Did you have a good day?"

Avoid: Leading Questions: Leading questions can be manipulative and may put your partner on the defensive. They can also create an unequal power dynamic in the relationship.

*Examples:*

- "Don't you think that was a stupid thing to do?"

- "Why do you always do that?"

- "Aren't you going to apologize?"

Tips for Effective Questioning in Romantic Relationships

While asking questions can be a powerful tool in building intimacy and communication in a relationship, there are some tips that can help to make your questioning more effective. Below are some tips to keep in mind when engaging in the art of questioning in your romantic relationship.

1. Be present: When asking questions, be fully present and attentive to your partner. Put aside distractions and focus on the conversation at hand.

2. Be curious: Approach questioning with a spirit of curiosity and interest in your partner's thoughts and feelings.

3. Avoid judgment: It's important to create a non-judgmental space for your partner to share. Try to avoid jumping to conclusions or making assumptions.

4. Listen actively: Listening is an essential component of effective questioning. Make sure you are actively listening to your partner's responses, and ask follow-up questions to demonstrate your interest.

5. Be patient: Sometimes, your partner may need time to process a question before responding. Allow them the time and space they need to formulate their thoughts and feelings.

6. Use "I" statements: When asking questions, try to frame them in a way that reflects your own feelings or experiences, rather than placing blame or judgment on your partner. This can help to foster a sense of safety and openness in the conversation.

7. Avoid defensiveness: It's natural to feel defensive when asked certain questions but try to avoid becoming defensive or shutting down the conversation. Instead, try to approach the conversation with an open mind and a willingness to learn and grow.

*Examples:*

- "I'm curious about how you feel when I do X. Can you tell me more about that?"

- "I feel hurt when you do Y. Can you help me understand why you did that?"

- "I'm struggling with Z, and I'd like to hear your thoughts on how we can work through it together."

## Summary

The art of questioning is a powerful tool for enhancing connection, communication, and understanding in romantic relationships. By asking open-ended, non-judgmental questions and approaching the conversation with curiosity and empathy, you can foster a sense of emotional safety and intimacy in your relationship. Remember to be patient, listen actively, and avoid becoming defensive, and you'll be well on your way to building a healthy, satisfying relationship.

# Lesson

# 7

# 200 Questions to Deepen Your Connections

Do you ever find yourself struggling to come up with meaningful conversation topics or wanting to deepen your connections with others? If so, you're not alone. One effective way to spark engaging conversations and build intimacy is by asking open-ended questions. These types of questions encourage the other person to share more than just a simple answer, but instead, provide insights into their thoughts, feelings, and experiences. To help get you started, we've compiled a list of 200 open-ended questions that you can use to enhance your relationships and spark meaningful conversations.

1. What are some of your favorite childhood memories?

2. What's something you've always wanted to try but haven't yet?

3. What are you most passionate about in life?

4. What motivates you to get up and start your day?

5. What are your greatest fears or anxieties?

6. What's something that you're currently struggling with?

7. What are your goals for the future?

8. Who has been the most influential person in your life, and why?

9. What's something you wish you could tell your younger self?

10. What's a skill or talent that you're proud of?

11. What's something you're curious about, but haven't had the chance to explore yet?

12. What's your favorite way to unwind after a long day?

13.      What's something you've learned recently that has surprised you?

14.      What's your favorite thing about your current job?

15.      What's something you've always wanted to ask me, but haven't yet?

16.      What's your favorite place you've ever traveled to?

17.      What's a book or movie that has had a significant impact on your life?

18.      What's something you believe strongly in, and why?

19.      What's a goal or dream that you've given up on?

20.      What's something you've done that you're particularly proud of?

21.      What's a place you've always wanted to visit, but haven't yet?

22.      What's your favorite way to spend time with loved ones?

23.      What's a lesson you've learned from a difficult experience?

24.      What's something that always makes you laugh?

25.      What's your favorite food or cuisine?

26.      What's something you've always wanted to learn, but haven't had the opportunity to?

27.      What's a memory you have that always brings a smile to your face?

28.      What's a hobby or interest that you're currently pursuing?

29.     What's something you find challenging about being in a relationship?

30.     What's a quality that you value in a friend?

31.     What's something you've been meaning to do, but keep putting off?

32.     What's a pet peeve or habit that you're working on improving?

33.     What's your favorite type of music or musician?

34.     What's a small act of kindness that someone has done for you that you'll never forget?

35.     What's a personal accomplishment that you're proud of?

36.     What's something you've always wanted to learn about a different culture?

37.     What's a fear you've overcome in the past?

38.     What's your favorite thing about yourself?

39.     What's a personal goal that you're currently working towards?

40.     What's a challenge you've overcome that has made you stronger?

41.     What's something you've always wanted to do, but haven't had the courage to try?

42.     What's a time when you've felt the most alive?

43.     What's something you're currently curious about?

44.     What's a movie or TV show that you could watch over and over again?

45.     What's something you're grateful for today?

46.     What's your favorite way to stay active or exercise?

47.     What's a quality that you value in a romantic partner?

48.     What's a place you've always wanted to live, but haven't had the opportunity to?

49.     What's a mistake you've made in the past that you've learned from?

50.     What's something you've always wanted to create, but haven't yet?

51.     What's a quote or mantra that inspires you?

52.     What's something you would do differently if you could go back in time?

53.     What's something that you're currently working on improving about yourself?

54.     What's a cause or issue that you're passionate about?

55.     What's something that you've always wanted to ask your parents?

56.     What's a trip that you've taken that has had a significant impact on your life?

57.     What's a time when you felt the most loved or supported by someone?

58.     What's a characteristic that you admire in others, but struggle to embody yourself?

59.     What's something you've done recently that has pushed you outside of your comfort zone?

60.     What's a habit or routine that you have that helps you feel grounded?

61.     What's something you're looking forward to in the next year?

62.     What's a gift that someone has given you that has meant a lot?

63.     What's something that you feel like you're currently missing in your life?

64.     What's a skill or talent that you would like to develop?

65.     What's your favorite way to celebrate milestones or accomplishments?

66.     What's something you're currently trying to let go of or move on from?

67.     What's a place in nature that you find particularly peaceful or rejuvenating?

68.     What's something you've always wanted to tell someone, but haven't had the chance to?

69.     What's a cause or issue that you wish more people knew about?

70.     What's a goal that you've accomplished that you initially thought was impossible?

71.     What's a song that always brings back memories or emotions for you?

72.     What's a quality that you value in yourself?

73.     What's something you've always wanted to say "yes" to, but haven't yet?

74.     What's a relationship that has had a significant impact on your life?

75.     What's something you're currently struggling to forgive yourself for?

76.     What's a book that has changed your perspective on something?

77.   What's a fear you have that you've never shared with anyone?

78.   What's something you're proud of, but don't often share with others?

79.   What's a trip that you're currently planning or dreaming of?

80.   What's a cause or issue that you feel personally connected to?

81.   What's a personal trait or quality that you've worked hard to develop?

82.   What's something you've always wanted to do for others, but haven't yet?

83.   What's a lesson you've learned from a difficult relationship?

84.   What's something that you've always wanted to try, but haven't had the time for?

85.   What's a dream or goal that you've had since childhood?

86.   What's a skill or talent that you've always wanted to teach someone?

87.   What's something that you're currently afraid of?

88.   What's a place that you feel most at peace or relaxed?

89.   What's a quote or saying that you live by?

90.   What's a fear that you've conquered in the past?

91.   What's something you've always wanted to do, but haven't had the resources for?

92.   What's a memory from your childhood that still resonates with you today?

93.     What's something that you're currently saving up for or working towards?

94.     What's a goal that you've set for yourself, but haven't yet achieved?

95.     What's a lesson that you've learned from a past romantic relationship?

96.     What's a trip that you've taken that has exceeded your expectations?

97.     What's something that you've always wanted to do with your partner, but haven't yet?

98.     What's a fear that you have that you'd like to overcome?

99.     What's something that you're currently feeling grateful for?

100.    What's something you've been curious about lately that you haven't had the chance to explore yet?

101.    What are some of the most important values you're looking for in a mate?

102.    What are some qualities that you think are essential for a successful relationship?

103.    What kind of personality traits are you attracted to?

104.    What kind of physical characteristics do you find attractive in a mate?

105.    What kind of sense of humor are you looking for in a mate?

106.    What are some deal breakers for you when it comes to a potential mate?

107.    What are some must-haves for you in a potential partner?

108.    What are some common interests you're looking for in a mate?

109.    What are some hobbies or activities that you'd like to share with your partner?

110.    What are some important factors when it comes to compatibility?

111.    What are some long-term goals you're looking for in a mate?

112.    What are some things that you'd like to achieve together as a couple?

113.    What are some qualities you're looking for in a life partner?

114.    What are some things that you'd like to experience with a mate?

115.    What are some things that you'd like to learn with a mate?

116.    What are some qualities you're looking for in a friend and a lover?

117.    What are some core values that you're looking for in a mate?

118.    What are some things that you'd like to teach your mate?

119.    What are some things that you'd like to learn from your mate?

120.    What are some things that you're willing to compromise on when it comes to a potential mate?

121.    What are some things that you're not willing to compromise on when it comes to a potential mate?

122.    What are some things that you think are important when it comes to communication in a relationship?

123.    What are some things that you think are important when it comes to intimacy in a relationship?

124.    What are some things that you think are important when it comes to trust in a relationship?

125.    What are some things that you think are important when it comes to honesty in a relationship?

126.    What are some things that you think are important when it comes to vulnerability in a relationship?

127.    What are some things that you think are important when it comes to emotional support in a relationship?

128.    What are some things that you think are important when it comes to physical affection in a relationship?

129.    What are some things that you think are important when it comes to emotional connection in a relationship?

130.    What are some things that you think are important when it comes to intellectual connection in a relationship?

131.    What are some things that you think are important when it comes to spiritual connection in a relationship?

132.    What are some things that you think are important when it comes to shared values in a relationship?

133.    What are some things that you think are important when it comes to mutual respect in a relationship?

134.    What are some things that you think are important when it comes to compromise in a relationship?

135.	What are some things that you think are important when it comes to supporting each other's goals in a relationship?

136.	What are some things that you think are important when it comes to growth in a relationship?

137.	What are some things that you think are important when it comes to adventure and exploration in a relationship?

138.	What are some things that you think are important when it comes to independence in a relationship?

139.	What are some things that you think are important when it comes to interdependence in a relationship?

140.	What are some things that you think are important when it comes to personal responsibility in a relationship?

141.	What are some things that you think are important when it comes to financial responsibility in a relationship?

142.	What are some things that you think are important when it comes to supporting each other's personal growth in a relationship?

143.	What are some things that you think are important when it comes to balancing individual needs and the needs of the relationship?

144.	What are some things that you think are important when it comes to conflict resolution in a relationship?

145.	What are some things that you think are important when it comes to showing affection and appreciation in a relationship?

146.   What are some things that you think are important when it comes to handling stress and challenges as a couple?

147.   What are some things that you think are important when it comes to having fun and enjoying life together as a couple?

148.   What are some things that you think are important when it comes to physical fitness and health as a couple?

149.   What are some things that you think are important when it comes to emotional intelligence and self-awareness as a couple?

150.   What are some things that you think are important when it comes to shared hobbies or interests?

151.   What are some things that you think are important when it comes to respecting each other's differences?

152.   What are some things that you think are important when it comes to having similar long-term goals?

153.   What are some things that you think are important when it comes to prioritizing time together as a couple?

154.   What are some things that you think are important when it comes to shared values around family and parenting?

155.   What are some things that you think are important when it comes to having a healthy work-life balance?

156.   What are some things that you think are important when it comes to feeling comfortable and safe with your partner?

157.	What are some things that you think are important when it comes to feeling supported in your personal and professional life?

158.	What are some things that you think are important when it comes to shared financial goals and planning?

159.	What are some things that you think are important when it comes to being able to have difficult conversations and work through disagreements?

160.	What are some things that you think are important when it comes to showing appreciation and gratitude for each other?

161.	What are some things that you think are important when it comes to maintaining a sense of independence and autonomy within the relationship?

162.	What are some things that you think are important when it comes to having a shared vision for the future?

163.	What are some things that you think are important when it comes to having a supportive and fulfilling sex life?

164.	What are some things that you think are important when it comes to having a shared understanding of the role of spirituality in the relationship?

165.	What are some things that you think are important when it comes to being able to have fun and laugh together?

166.	What are some things that you think are important when it comes to feeling accepted and loved for who you are?

167.	What are some things that you think are important when it comes to having a sense of adventure and trying new things together?

168.  What are some things that you think are important when it comes to having shared values around social and environmental issues?

169.  What are some things that you think are important when it comes to being able to communicate openly and honestly about your emotions and feelings?

170.  What are some things that you think are important when it comes to having a shared understanding of the role of family and friends in the relationship?

171.  What are some things that you think are important when it comes to having a shared sense of purpose or mission in life?

172.  What are some things that you think are important when it comes to feeling heard and understood by your partner?

173.  What are some things that you think are important when it comes to respecting each other's boundaries and personal space?

174.  What are some things that you think are important when it comes to having a shared sense of humor and being able to laugh together?

175.  What are some things that you think are important when it comes to having a shared understanding of the role of religion in the relationship?

176.  What are some things that you think are important when it comes to being able to trust and rely on your partner?

177.  What are some things that you think are important when it comes to being able to express your needs and desires to your partner?

178.  What are some things that you think are important when it comes to having a shared sense of style or aesthetic?

179.    What are some things that you think are important when it comes to having shared values around travel and adventure?

180.    What are some things that you think are important when it comes to being able to support each other's career goals and aspirations?

181.    What are some things that you think are important when it comes to having a shared understanding of the role of money in the relationship?

182.    What are some things that you think are important when it comes to having a shared sense of purpose or mission in the relationship?

183.    What are some things that you think are important when it comes to being able to express and receive love in different ways?

184.    What are some things that you think are important when it comes to respecting each other's cultural backgrounds and traditions?

185.    What are some things that you think are important when it comes to having a shared sense of adventure and willingness to try new things?

186.    What are some things that you think are important when it comes to having a shared understanding of the role of education in the relationship?

187.    What are some things that you think are important when it comes to being able to forgive and move forward after disagreements or conflicts?

188.    What are some things that you think are important when it comes to having shared values around social justice and equity?

189.    What are some things that you think are important when it comes to being able to prioritize self-care and mental health within the relationship?

190.    What are some things that you think are important when it comes to having a shared understanding of the role of technology in the relationship?

191.    What are some things that you think are important when it comes to being able to have deep and meaningful conversations about life and the world?

192.    What are some things that you think are important when it comes to having a shared understanding of the role of politics in the relationship?

193.    What are some things that you think are important when it comes to being able to have open and honest communication about sexual preferences and desires?

194.    What are some things that you think are important when it comes to having a shared understanding of the role of humor in the relationship?

195.    What are some things that you think are important when it comes to being able to celebrate each other's accomplishments and milestones?

196.    What are some things that you think are important when it comes to having a shared understanding of the role of spirituality in the relationship?

197.    What are some things that you think are important when it comes to being able to support each other through difficult times and challenges?

198.    What are some things that you think are important when it comes to having a shared understanding of the role of family and community in the relationship?

199.    What are some things that you think are important when it comes to having a shared understanding of the role of gender roles and expectations in the relationship?

200.    What are some things that you think are important when it comes to having a shared understanding of the role of gender roles and expectations in the relationship?

**Summary**

Using open-ended questions as a communication tool can help you create deeper connections with other people and foster engaging conversations. By asking these types of questions, you can gain insight into the thoughts, feelings, and experiences of those around you, and create a more meaningful and fulfilling relationship. Asking thoughtful questions can lead to an exchange of ideas and a greater understanding of each other, allowing you to establish stronger relationships and build a more supportive community.

Lesson

# 8

# Love or Leap: Relationship Deal Breakers

Entering a romantic relationship or marriage is a significant decision that requires careful consideration and evaluation. While love and attraction are crucial elements in forming a lasting relationship, it's equally essential to pay attention to potential warning signs or red flags that may indicate incompatibility or ineligibility. Identifying and addressing these issues early on can prevent heartache, disappointment, or worse, abuse, and trauma.

In this section, we've compiled a comprehensive checklist of 300 red flags, warning signs, and deal breakers that you should be aware of when considering marriage or a relationship. Whether you're single, dating, or engaged, this list can help you identify potential issues and make informed decisions about your future.

## Red Flags

☐ Disrespectful behavior towards you or others.

☐ Controlling behavior.

☐ Lack of trust or transparency.

☐ Excessive jealousy.

☐ Constant criticism.

☐ Refusal to compromise.

☐ History of infidelity.

☐ Addiction to drugs or alcohol.

☐ Financial irresponsibility.

☐ Inability to communicate effectively.

- ☐ Lack of emotional support.

- ☐ Incompatible goals and values.

- ☐ Refusal to take responsibility for their actions.

- ☐ Emotional or physical abuse.

- ☐ Refusal to apologize or admit fault.

- ☐ Poor conflict resolution skills.

- ☐ Different religious beliefs.

- ☐ History of criminal behavior.

- ☐ Difficulty managing anger.

- ☐ Refusal to seek help or therapy.

- ☐ Avoidance of discussing the future together.

- ☐ Lack of respect for boundaries.

- ☐ Constant need for attention.

- ☐ Overly critical of your family and friends.

- ☐ Selfish behavior.

- ☐ Prioritizing their needs over yours.

- ☐ Negative attitude towards marriage or commitment.

☐ Lack of intimacy or interest in sex.

☐ Disinterest in your hobbies or passions.

☐ Refusal to compromise on major decisions.

☐ Refusal to attend premarital counseling.

☐ Dishonesty or lack of transparency about their past.

☐ Inability to maintain a job or career.

☐ Refusal to communicate their feelings.

☐ Difficulty expressing empathy towards others.

☐ Lack of emotional intelligence.

☐ Inability to apologize sincerely.

☐ Demonstrating narcissistic traits.

☐ Refusal to respect your opinion.

☐ History of being emotionally unavailable.

☐ Blaming others for their mistakes.

☐ Constant need for validation or approval.

☐ Ignoring your thoughts or feelings.

☐ Lack of gratitude or appreciation.

☐ Refusal to make compromises in their lifestyle.

☐ History of being unfaithful in past relationships.

☐ Refusal to discuss finances openly and honestly.

☐ Refusal to discuss children and parenting styles.

☐ History of being emotionally manipulative.

☐ Disrespectful or dismissive towards your culture or heritage.

☐ Inability to express vulnerability.

☐ Lack of common interests or hobbies.

☐ Refusal to discuss family planning and contraception.

☐ Inability to handle stress or anxiety.

☐ Refusal to make an effort to get along with your family and friends.

☐ Lack of ambition or drive.

☐ Refusal to seek medical help for physical or mental health issues.

☐ History of not taking responsibility for their actions.

☐ Refusal to respect your privacy.

☐ Lack of emotional stability.

☐ History of being emotionally abusive in past relationships.

- ☐ Refusal to share responsibilities in the relationship.

- ☐ Lack of empathy towards animals or pets.

- ☐ Refusal to attend family events or holidays.

- ☐ History of lying or being deceitful.

- ☐ Refusal to compromise on household chores and responsibilities.

- ☐ Inability to maintain friendships.

- ☐ Lack of respect towards your career or job.

- ☐ Refusal to discuss personal values and beliefs.

- ☐ Inability to admit mistakes.

- ☐ History of being verbally abusive in past relationships.

- ☐ Refusal to support your personal growth and development.

- ☐ Lack of emotional maturity.

- ☐ Refusal to communicate about important issues.

- ☐ Demonstrating manipulative behavior.

- ☐ Lack of interest in spending quality time together.

- ☐ Refusal to make time for your hobbies or passions.

- ☐ Lack of sexual compatibility.

☐ History be being financially dependent on their partners

☐ Refusal to compromise on lifestyle choices, such as living arrangements or travel plans.

☐ Demonstrating possessive behavior.

☐ Lack of interest in shared experiences or adventures.

☐ Refusal to acknowledge their own flaws or shortcomings.

☐ Inability to take constructive criticism.

☐ Demonstrating a lack of empathy towards marginalized groups.

☐ Refusal to discuss important life decisions.

☐ Demonstrating a lack of respect towards your time and schedule.

☐ Refusal to work on issues in the relationship.

☐ Lack of emotional availability.

☐ Refusal to address past trauma or emotional baggage.

☐ Demonstrating avoidant behavior towards conflicts.

☐ Lack of accountability for their own actions.

☐ Demonstrating controlling behavior towards finances.

☐ Refusal to address issues with communication.

☐ Lack of emotional intimacy in the relationship.

☐  Demonstrating passive-aggressive behavior.

☐  Refusal to take responsibility for their own happiness.

☐  Demonstrating an unwillingness to compromise on cultural differences.

☐  Lack of effort in maintaining physical intimacy.

☐  Refusal to work on personal growth and development.

## Warning Signs

☐  Refusal to acknowledge their own privilege or biases.

☐  Demonstrating a lack of interest in your thoughts or opinions.

☐  Refusal to take responsibility for their own role in conflicts.

☐  Demonstrating a lack of effort in building a sense of community with each other.

☐  Refusal to acknowledge the importance of shared values in the relationship.

☐  Demonstrating a lack of appreciation for your efforts or contributions.

☐  Refusal to acknowledge the importance of shared goals in the relationship.

☐  Demonstrating a lack of curiosity or interest in learning about your family or background.

☐  Refusal to acknowledge the importance of honesty in the relationship.

☐  Demonstrating a lack of effort in building a strong emotional connection.

☐  Refusal to acknowledge the impact of past traumas on the relationship.

☐ Demonstrating a lack of accountability for their own emotional reactions.

☐ Refusal to acknowledge the importance of self-awareness in the relationship.

☐ Demonstrating a lack of empathy towards your struggles or challenges.

☐ Refusal to acknowledge the importance of growth and change in the relationship.

☐ Demonstrating a lack of respect towards your friends or loved ones.

☐ Refusal to acknowledge the importance of healthy communication in the relationship.

☐ Demonstrating a lack of effort in building a sense of shared purpose or vision.

☐ Refusal to acknowledge the importance of compromise in the relationship.

☐ Demonstrating a lack of trust towards your partner.

☐ Refusal to acknowledge the importance of forgiveness in the relationship.

☐ Demonstrating a lack of effort in building a sense of shared meaning or values.

☐ Refusal to acknowledge the importance of vulnerability in the relationship.

☐ Demonstrating a lack of willingness to try new things together.

☐ Refusal to acknowledge the importance of mutual respect in the relationship.

☐ Demonstrating a lack of effort in building a sense of shared humor or joy.

☐ Refusal to acknowledge the importance of physical touch in the relationship.

☐ Demonstrating a lack of willingness to learn from past mistakes or failures.

☐ Refusal to acknowledge the importance of shared responsibility in the relationship.

☐ Demonstrating a lack of effort in building a sense of shared appreciation or gratitude.

☐ Refusal to acknowledge the importance of shared experiences in the relationship.

☐ Demonstrating a lack of willingness to compromise on daily routines or habits.

☐ Refusal to acknowledge the importance of quality time in the relationship.

☐ Demonstrating a lack of effort in building a sense of shared curiosity or interest.

☐ Refusal to acknowledge the importance of emotional support in the relationship.

☐ Demonstrating a lack of willingness to acknowledge the impact of past relationships on the relationship.

☐ Refusal to acknowledge the importance of personal growth and development in the relationship.

☐ Demonstrating a lack of effort in building a sense of shared adventure or exploration.

☐ Refusal to acknowledge the importance of open-mindedness in the relationship.

☐ Demonstrating a lack of willingness to acknowledge the importance of self-care in the relationship.

☐ Refusal to acknowledge the importance of shared traditions or rituals in the relationship.

☐ Demonstrating a lack of effort in building a sense of shared spirituality or belief.

☐ Refusal to acknowledge the importance of shared hobbies or interests in the relationship.

☐ Demonstrating a lack of willingness to acknowledge the importance of mutual support in the relationship.

☐ Refusal to acknowledge the importance of shared growth and transformation in the relationship.

☐ Lack of trust or dishonesty in the relationship.

☐ Demonstrating toxic behavior, such as gaslighting or manipulation.

☐ Refusal to work on personal growth and development.

☐ Demonstrating abusive behavior, either physical or emotional.

☐ Significant differences in religious or political beliefs.

☐ Refusal to address past trauma or emotional baggage.

☐ Demonstrating avoidant behavior towards conflicts.

☐ Lack of communication or poor communication skills.

☐ Disrespecting your values or beliefs.

☐ Refusal to acknowledge their own flaws or shortcomings.

☐ Demonstrating controlling behavior towards finances.

☐ Refusal to work on issues in the relationship.

☐ Demonstrating a lack of empathy towards marginalized groups.

☐ Lack of emotional availability.

☐ Demonstrating possessive behavior.

☐ Refusal to compromise on lifestyle choices, such as living arrangements or travel plans.

☐ Demonstrating a lack of respect towards your time and schedule.

☐ Lack of effort in maintaining physical intimacy.

☐ Refusal to take responsibility for their own happiness.

☐ Demonstrating an unwillingness to compromise on cultural differences.

☐ Refusal to discuss important life decisions.

☐ Lack of emotional intimacy in the relationship.

☐ Demonstrating passive-aggressive behavior.

☐ Inability to take constructive criticism.

☐ Significant differences in parenting styles or desires for children.

☐ Demonstrating a lack of interest in your life or hobbies.

☐ Refusal to apologize or make amends when necessary.

☐ Demonstrating a lack of ambition or motivation.

☐ Refusal to acknowledge the impact of their actions on others.

☐ Demonstrating a lack of generosity or kindness towards others.

☐ Refusal to set boundaries with family or friends.

☐ Demonstrating a lack of responsibility or reliability.

☐ Significant differences in lifestyle or spending habits.

☐ Refusal to acknowledge the seriousness of mental health concerns.

☐ Demonstrating a lack of appreciation or gratitude.

☐ Refusal to take ownership of their mistakes.

☐ Demonstrating a lack of consideration towards your feelings.

☐ Inability to handle stress or conflict in a healthy way.

☐ Demonstrating a lack of curiosity or interest in learning new things.

☐ Refusal to compromise on career goals or ambitions.

☐ Demonstrating a lack of compassion towards animals or the environment.

☐ Refusal to address issues with addiction or substance abuse.

☐ Demonstrating a lack of interest in personal hygiene or self-care.

☐ Refusal to seek professional help for mental health concerns.

☐ Demonstrating a lack of respect towards your boundaries.

☐ Refusal to acknowledge the importance of healthy boundaries.

☐ Demonstrating a lack of effort in building a strong friendship.

☐ Refusal to acknowledge the importance of intimacy in the relationship.

☐ Demonstrating a lack of accountability for their own actions.

☐ Refusal to acknowledge their impact on the relationship.

☐ Demonstrating a lack of commitment to the relationship.

☐ Refusal to take responsibility for their own emotional well-being.

☐ Demonstrating a lack of interest in shared experiences or adventures.

☐ Refusal to respect your privacy or personal space.

☐ Demonstrating a lack of flexibility

## Deal-Breakers

☐ Physical or emotional abuse

☐ Cheating or infidelity

☐ Refusal to communicate or address issues

☐ Fundamental differences in values or beliefs

☐ Dishonesty or deception

☐ Lack of trust

☐ Refusal to compromise

☐ Disrespectful behavior

☐ Financial irresponsibility

☐ Lack of emotional support

☐ Refusal to take responsibility for actions

☐ Incompatibility in life goals

☐ Substance abuse or addiction

☐ Lack of intimacy or affection

☐ Poor hygiene or cleanliness

☐ Lack of personal hygiene

☐ Refusal to work on personal growth or improvement

☐ Constant arguing or fighting

☐ Refusal to respect boundaries

☐ Inability to resolve conflicts

☐ Significant differences in sex drive or sexual preferences

☐ Significant differences in cultural or religious backgrounds

☐ Refusal to apologize or make amends

☐ Constant negativity or pessimism

☐ Extreme jealousy or possessiveness

☐ Refusal to seek professional help when necessary

- ☐ Emotional immaturity or instability

- ☐ Refusal to compromise on major decisions

- ☐ Refusal to acknowledge the importance of trust in the relationship

- ☐ Lack of respect for each other's families or friends

- ☐ Extreme clinginess or neediness

- ☐ Refusal to acknowledge the importance of personal space

- ☐ Refusal to acknowledge the importance of shared responsibility

- ☐ Lack of interest or effort in spending time together

- ☐ Refusal to acknowledge the importance of personal growth and development

- ☐ Significant differences in lifestyle or interests

- ☐ Refusal to acknowledge the importance of healthy communication

- ☐ Dishonesty about past or present situations

- ☐ Refusal to acknowledge the importance of forgiveness

- ☐ Different parenting styles or views on having children

- ☐ Refusal to acknowledge the importance of shared experiences

- ☐ Refusal to acknowledge the impact of past relationships on the current one

- ☐ Lack of emotional intelligence or empathy

- ☐ Refusal to acknowledge the importance of quality time

- ☐ Inability to handle stress or pressure

- ☐ Refusal to acknowledge the importance of mutual support

- ☐ Significant differences in social or political beliefs

- ☐ Refusal to acknowledge the importance of compromise

- ☐ Extreme or unpredictable mood swings

- ☐ Refusal to acknowledge the importance of mutual respect

- ☐ Refusal to acknowledge the importance of shared traditions or rituals

- ☐ Different views on marriage or commitment

- ☐ Refusal to acknowledge the importance of physical attraction

- ☐ Refusal to acknowledge the importance of emotional intimacy

- ☐ Refusal to acknowledge the importance of intellectual compatibility

- ☐ Lack of ambition or drive

- ☐ Refusal to acknowledge the importance of shared goals

- ☐ Significant age difference

- ☐ Refusal to acknowledge the importance of personal responsibility

- ☐ Inability to control anger or frustration

- ☐ Refusal to acknowledge the importance of emotional honesty

- ☐ Refusal to acknowledge the importance of emotional vulnerability

- ☐ Refusal to acknowledge the importance of self-care

- ☐ Refusal to acknowledge the importance of open-mindedness

- ☐ Different levels of education or intelligence

- ☐ Refusal to acknowledge the importance of shared spirituality or beliefs

- ☐ Refusal to acknowledge the importance of personal growth

- ☐ Different career paths or goals

- ☐ Refusal to acknowledge the importance of trustworthiness

- ☐ Refusal to acknowledge the importance of physical and emotional safety

- ☐ Refusal to acknowledge the importance of healthy boundaries

- ☐ Different views on personal hygiene

- ☐ Refusal to acknowledge the importance of emotional support

- ☐ Refusal to acknowledge the importance of quality communication

- ☐ Significant differences in emotional expression or communication styles

- ☐ Refusal to acknowledge the importance of shared responsibility in household tasks

- ☐ Refusal to acknowledge the importance of mutual respect for each other's feelings

☐ Refusal to acknowledge the importance of mutual support in difficult times

☐ Refusal to acknowledge the importance of shared interests or hobbies

☐ Refusal to acknowledge the importance of honesty in all aspects of the relationship

☐ Refusal to acknowledge the importance of maintaining individual identities within the relationship

☐ Refusal to acknowledge the importance of shared decision-making

☐ Refusal to acknowledge the importance of healthy conflict resolution

☐ Refusal to acknowledge the importance of compromise in personal preferences

☐ Refusal to acknowledge the importance of a healthy work-life balance

☐ Refusal to acknowledge the importance of shared values regarding social issues

☐ Refusal to acknowledge the importance of consistent effort in maintaining the relationship

☐ Refusal to acknowledge the importance of shared responsibilities in financial matters

☐ Refusal to acknowledge the importance of addressing issues in a timely and respectful manner

☐ Refusal to acknowledge the importance of mutual trust in all aspects of the relationship

☐ Refusal to acknowledge the importance of mutual support for personal growth and development

☐ Refusal to acknowledge the importance of respecting each other's privacy and personal space

☐ Refusal to acknowledge the importance of mutual commitment to the relationship

☐ Refusal to acknowledge the importance of mutual acceptance and celebration of differences

☐ Refusal to acknowledge the importance of shared communication around sexual preferences and boundaries

☐ Refusal to acknowledge the importance of mutual support in achieving personal and shared goals

☐ Refusal to acknowledge the importance of regular date nights or quality time spent together

☐ Refusal to acknowledge the importance of consistent effort in building and maintaining intimacy

☐ Refusal to acknowledge the importance of mutual respect for each other's feelings, opinions, and boundaries.

☐ Refusal to acknowledge the importance of apologizing and making amends for mistakes or wrongdoing in the relationship.

## Summary

Entering a romantic relationship or marriage requires careful consideration and evaluation, and it's important to pay attention to potential warning signs or red flags that may indicate incompatibility or ineligibility. Our comprehensive list of 300 red flags, warning signs, and deal breakers can help you identify potential issues and make informed decisions about your future. Remember that this list is not exhaustive, and every relationship is unique. However, by being aware of these warning signs and addressing them early on, you can potentially prevent heartache, disappointment, or worse, abuse, and trauma. Ultimately, your safety, happiness, and well-being should be your top priority in any relationship.

# 9

# Managing Mental Health & Relationships

# Sexual Healing

Mental illness affects millions of people worldwide and can have a significant impact on an individual's personal and social life. It can be particularly challenging for those who are pursuing intimate or marital relationships. Many individuals may feel compelled to enter into relationships despite struggling with mental health concerns, believing that a relationship will help them cope. However, research suggests that seeking help for mental illness before entering into intimate relationships can significantly improve the well-being of both partners. This lesson aims to highlight the importance of taking care of oneself first and seeking help for mental illness before pursuing intimate or marital relationships.

The decision to seek help for mental illness can be challenging, but it is crucial to prioritize one's mental health. Seeking help can help individuals manage their symptoms, build healthy relationships, and develop coping strategies to manage stress and avoid triggers that may exacerbate their condition. By doing so, individuals can focus on their own well-being and address any underlying issues that may interfere with their ability to maintain a successful relationship.

Here are the 7 reasons why it is important to seek help for mental illness before pursuing intimate or marital relationships:

1. To Manage Symptoms: Seeking help can provide individuals with the tools and resources needed to manage their mental health symptoms effectively. This can prevent symptoms from negatively affecting their relationships.

2. To Develop Coping Strategies: Mental illness can make it difficult to cope with stress, which can put a strain on relationships. Seeking help can provide individuals with coping strategies to manage stress and improve their relationships.

3. To Build Healthy Relationships: Seeking help for mental illness can help individuals develop healthy relationships. This includes developing communication skills, setting boundaries, and building trust, which are crucial for any successful relationship.

4. To Avoid Triggers: Mental illness can be triggered by various factors, including stress, relationship problems, and life changes. Seeking help can help individuals identify and avoid these triggers, reducing the risk of a relapse.

5. To Improve Self-Esteem: Mental illness can affect an individual's self-esteem, which can make it challenging to develop healthy relationships. Seeking help can improve self-esteem, leading to more fulfilling relationships.

6. To Prevent Dependency: Mental illness can lead to codependency, where individuals rely on their partner for emotional support. Seeking help can prevent codependency and promote healthy independence in relationships.

7. To Reduce the Risk of Relationship Breakdown: Mental illness can put a significant strain on relationships, leading to breakdowns. Seeking help can reduce the risk of relationship breakdowns and improve the chances of maintaining healthy, fulfilling relationships.

## Mental Trauma and Its Impact on Relationships

Mental trauma can have a profound impact on a person's life, affecting their relationships, work, and overall well-being. Trauma is an emotional response to an event or series of events that are deeply distressing or disturbing. It can be caused by a wide range of experiences, including physical, emotional, or sexual abuse, natural disasters, accidents, or witnessing violent or traumatic events. While trauma affects individuals differently, it often results in a range of symptoms, such as anxiety, depression, sleep disturbances, and difficulties with interpersonal relationships.

When individuals experience mental trauma, it can affect their ability to form and maintain healthy relationships. Trauma can lead to feelings of shame, guilt, and worthlessness, making it challenging for individuals to trust others and feel safe in their relationships. Additionally, trauma can impact communication skills, leading to misunderstandings and conflicts within relationships.

Here are some ways mental trauma can impact relationships:

1. Trust Issues: Individuals who have experienced mental trauma may struggle to trust others, making it challenging to form and maintain healthy relationships. Trauma can create a sense of mistrust and fear, leading individuals to avoid close relationships or engage in self-destructive behaviors.

2. Fear of Abandonment: Trauma can lead individuals to fear being abandoned or rejected, making it challenging to develop secure and healthy attachments with others. Individuals may become overly clingy or avoidant in relationships, leading to difficulties with intimacy and connection.

3. Communication Difficulties: Trauma can impact communication skills, leading to misunderstandings and conflicts within relationships. Individuals may struggle to express themselves effectively, leading to feelings of frustration and isolation.

4. Emotional Instability: Trauma can lead to emotional instability, with individuals experiencing intense and unpredictable emotions. This can put a significant strain on relationships, as partners may struggle to understand or cope with the individual's emotional responses.

5. Codependency: Individuals who have experienced mental trauma may become overly dependent on their partner for emotional support. This can lead to codependent relationships, where one partner takes on a caretaking role, leading to imbalanced and unhealthy dynamics.

6. Avoidance Behaviors: Trauma can lead individuals to engage in avoidance behaviors, such as withdrawing from relationships or using substances to cope. These behaviors can further impact relationships, leading to feelings of abandonment and frustration.

7. Sexual Dysfunction: Trauma can also impact sexual function, leading to difficulties with intimacy and sexual relationships. Individuals may experience sexual dysfunctions such as decreased libido or difficulty achieving orgasm, leading to additional relationship challenges.

When it comes to mental illness in the U.S., here are some interesting statistics:

- According to the National Institute of Mental Health (NIMH), an estimated 51.5 million adults (ages 18 and older) in the United States have a mental illness in any given year. This represents about 20% of the adult population.

- The most common mental illnesses in the U.S. are anxiety disorders, which affect an estimated 31.1% of adults at some point in their lives, and major depression, which affects an estimated 17.3% of adults at some point in their lives.

- The Substance Abuse and Mental Health Services Administration (SAMHSA) reports that an estimated 19.4% of U.S. adults (ages 18 and older) experienced a mental illness in 2020, with rates being higher among young adults aged 18-25.

- NIMH reports that an estimated 4.4% of U.S. adults experience serious mental illness (SMI) in any given year, which is defined as a mental illness that significantly impairs functioning and requires treatment.

- Among children and adolescents (ages 6-17), an estimated 9.4% have a serious emotional disturbance (SED) that significantly impacts daily functioning and requires treatment, according to SAMHSA.

This means that there is more of a possibility than not that yourself, the person that you are considering to be your mate, or both of you are dealing with some form of diagnosed or undiagnosed mental illness, impairment or trauma. Now, the decision to take medication for mental disorders is a personal choice. However, as this book is about dig deep to uncover risk, it is important to understand the potential risks of not taking medication as prescribed for mental disorders.

Here are some possible risks:

1. Worsening symptoms: Not taking medication for a mental disorder can lead to a worsening of symptoms, including increased anxiety, depression, mood swings, and psychotic symptoms. This can negatively impact an individual's overall functioning and quality of life.

2. Impaired daily functioning: Mental disorders can interfere with an individual's ability to perform daily tasks such as working, studying, socializing, and caring for themselves. Not taking medication can lead to a decrease in the ability to perform these tasks and can lead to more severe symptoms.

3. Increased risk of hospitalization: If mental health symptoms become severe, an individual may require hospitalization for stabilization and treatment. Not taking medication can increase the risk of hospitalization for mental health concerns.

4. Increased risk of suicide: Some mental disorders such as depression and bipolar disorder can increase the risk of suicide. Not taking medication can increase this risk and make it more difficult to manage suicidal thoughts or behaviors.

5. Negative impact on relationships: Mental disorders can impact an individual's ability to form and maintain healthy relationships. Not taking medication can lead to a worsening of symptoms and make it more challenging to communicate and connect with others.

6. Increased risk of substance abuse: Not taking medication for mental disorders can lead to an increased risk of substance abuse as individuals may use substances to cope with symptoms.

It is important to note that not everyone with a mental disorder requires medication, and there may be alternative treatments that can be effective. However, if medication is prescribed, it is important to take it as directed by a qualified healthcare provider to manage symptoms effectively and reduce potential risks.

If you or someone you know is struggling with mental health concerns, it is important to seek support from a qualified healthcare provider or mental health professional.

In conclusion, seeking help for mental illness and trauma before pursuing intimate or marital relationships is crucial to prioritize one's mental health and promote overall well-being. By managing symptoms, developing coping strategies, building healthy relationships, avoiding triggers, improving self-esteem, preventing dependency, and reducing the risk of relationship breakdown, individuals can take care of themselves first and ensure successful relationships. It is essential to seek help when needed and address any underlying mental health concerns to achieve and maintain healthy, fulfilling relationships.

# 10

# Dynamic Partnership Characteristics

Developing Healthy Relationship Skills. In this lesson, we will explore the essential characteristics of a good man and a good woman and provide checklists to help you assess your own readiness for a relationship. We will also offer a variety of exercises to help with personal development and growth, such as deep self-reflection, uncovering motivations for commitment, discussing important relationship topics, and assessing financial and emotional readiness for various life stages. Additionally, we will delve into the unique challenges of stepparenting and offer a self-assessment quiz to determine your readiness for a relationship. By the end of this lesson, you will have a better understanding of what it takes to build healthy relationships and make informed decisions about love and commitment. Let's get started!

The term "good man" is often used to describe someone who possesses a variety of positive attributes, such as honesty, integrity, kindness, and compassion. However, defining what makes a man "good" is not always easy. In this article, we will explore 10 characteristics that are commonly associated with being a good man. These characteristics are not listed in any particular order, as different people may prioritize certain traits over others.

1. Empathy: The ability to understand and share the feelings of others is an essential characteristic of a good man. Empathy allows men to connect with those around them on a deeper level and show compassion towards others. According to a study conducted by the University of Michigan, men who exhibit higher levels of empathy report greater life satisfaction and overall well-being.

2. Integrity: Integrity is a crucial characteristic of a good man. It involves being honest and having strong moral principles, even in the face of adversity. Men with high levels of integrity are respected and admired by others. In fact, a study conducted by Harvard Business Review found that 84% of employees consider integrity to be the most important trait in their leaders.

3. Responsibility: A good man takes responsibility for his actions and is accountable for the consequences. This means owning up to mistakes and working to make things right. According to a survey by the American Psychological Association, men who take responsibility for their actions report higher levels of life satisfaction and well-being.

4. Kindness: Kindness is another essential characteristic of a good man. Being kind involves showing compassion and generosity towards others, regardless of their background or circumstances. In a study published in the Journal of Positive Psychology, researchers found that acts of kindness can boost happiness levels in both the giver and receiver.

5. Respect: Respect is a crucial aspect of any healthy relationship, and it is especially important for men to demonstrate respect towards women. A good man treats others with respect, regardless of their gender, ethnicity, or social status. According to a study published in the Journal of Social and Personal Relationships, men who demonstrate higher levels of respect towards their partners report greater relationship satisfaction.

6. Humility: Humility is an underrated but important characteristic of a good man. It involves recognizing one's own limitations and shortcomings and being willing to learn from others. Men who exhibit higher levels of humility are more likely to be open-minded and empathetic towards others. According to a study published in the Journal of Positive Psychology, humble individuals report greater life satisfaction and well-being.

7. Courage: Courage is another essential characteristic of a good man. It involves facing one's fears and taking action in the face of adversity. Men who exhibit higher levels of courage are more likely to succeed in life and be respected by others. In fact, a study published in the Journal of Positive Psychology found that courage is a key factor in achieving success and happiness.

8. Communication: Effective communication is an important characteristic of a good man. It involves being able to express one's thoughts and feelings clearly and respectfully. Men who communicate effectively are more likely to have healthy relationships and be successful in both their personal and professional lives. According to a study conducted by the University of Minnesota, couples who communicate effectively report higher levels of relationship satisfaction.

9. Generosity: Generosity is another important characteristic of a good man. It involves being willing to give to others without expecting anything in return. Men who exhibit higher levels of generosity are more likely to be respected and admired by others. In fact, a study published in the Journal of Happiness Studies found that people who engage in acts of generosity report higher levels of happiness and life satisfaction.

10. Self-Reflection: Finally, a good man engages in self-reflection and introspection. This involves taking the time to examine one's own thoughts and behaviors and being open to self-improvement. Men who engage in self-reflection are more likely to develop a deeper understanding of themselves and those around them. According to a study published in the Journal of Personality and Social Psychology, individuals who engage in self-reflection are more likely to experience personal growth and development.

In conclusion, being a good man is not just about exhibiting a single characteristic, but rather a combination of many positive traits. These 10 characteristics, which include empathy, integrity, responsibility, kindness, respect, humility, courage, communication, generosity, and self-reflection, are all important aspects of being a good man. By working to develop these characteristics, men can become better partners, friends, and leaders, and contribute positively to society as a whole.

# Good Man (The Checklist)

Women looking for good men often struggle to identify the characteristics of such a man, so here's a checklist to help you identify these elements in a potential partner. It may seem straightforward, but it can be challenging for many women to identify these qualities in a man. Due to toxic masculinity and societal expectations that men should be dominant and unemotional, it may be difficult to distinguish between genuine goodness and performance. According to researcher Terri Orbuch, "Many men appear good on the surface but lack the qualities that make them truly good men."

A recent survey by Match.com found that 70% of women have difficulty recognizing the signs of a good partner. Women, however, can identify the traits of a good man with the help of this checklist and establish healthy, fulfilling relationships based on these traits.

To ensure successful, meaningful relationships, it is essential for women to understand what makes a "good man", and this checklist can help to ensure they make an informed decision.

## 10 Characteristics of A Good Man

### 1. Empathy:

- Does he actively listen and show genuine interest in what you have to say?
- Does he demonstrate concern for others, such as family, friends, or even strangers?
- Does he exhibit emotional intelligence and understanding?

### 2. Integrity:

- Does he stick to his word and follow through on his promises?
- Does he admit to his mistakes and take accountability for his actions?
- Does he exhibit consistency in his values and behavior?

3. **Responsibility:**

- Does he take ownership of his life and actively work towards his goals?

- Does he take responsibility for his actions and their consequences?

- Does he exhibit reliability in his commitments?

4. **Kindness:**

- Does he show kindness towards you and others?

- Does he exhibit empathy and compassion towards others?

- Does he engage in acts of kindness without expecting anything in return?

5. **Respect:**

- Does he treat you with respect and dignity?

- Does he show respect towards your family, friends, and others in your life?

- Does he exhibit respect towards people from different backgrounds and cultures?

6. **Humility:**

- Does he show humility in acknowledging his limitations and faults?

- Is he open to feedback and willing to learn from others?

- Does he avoid arrogance and a sense of superiority?

7. **Courage:**

- Does he exhibit courage in the face of challenges and adversity?

- Is he willing to take risks and pursue his goals despite potential obstacles?

- Does he exhibit bravery in standing up for what is right and just?

8. **Communication:**

- Does he communicate effectively and respectfully?

- Does he actively listen and seek to understand your perspective?

- Does he express his thoughts and feelings clearly and honestly?

9. **Generosity:**

- Does he exhibit generosity towards you and others?

- Does he engage in acts of kindness and giving without expecting anything in return?

- Does he show a willingness to share his time, resources, and energy?

10. **Self-Reflection:**

- Does he engage in self-reflection and introspection?

- Is he open to feedback and willing to learn from his mistakes?

- Does he exhibit a desire for personal growth and development?

While these characteristics are not the only factors to consider when choosing a partner, they can serve as a helpful guide in identifying qualities that are important in a good man. By using this checklist, women can identify potential partners who embody these characteristics and build healthy, fulfilling relationships.

## Unleashing Her Potential: The Characteristics of a Strong and Empowered Woman

**Introduction:**

The term "good woman" can have different meanings depending on the individual's cultural and societal background. However, there are certain characteristics that are universally accepted as being important traits of a good woman. These characteristics include qualities such as honesty, loyalty, kindness, and respect. In this article, we will discuss 10 characteristics that define a good woman and why they are essential for a fulfilling and meaningful life.

1. Honesty: Honesty is the foundation of any healthy relationship, and it is an essential quality of a good woman. Being honest with oneself and others creates a sense of trust and security in relationships. According to a survey conducted by the American Psychological Association, 50% of Americans believe that honesty is the most essential quality in a relationship.

2. Kindness: Kindness is an act of empathy and compassion towards others. A good woman demonstrates kindness in her daily interactions with others, making them feel valued and appreciated. Studies have shown that practicing acts of kindness can improve overall well-being and lead to a more positive outlook on life.

3. Independence: An independent woman is confident in her abilities and can take care of herself. She is not afraid to take risks and pursue her dreams, even if it means stepping outside of her comfort zone. According to a report by the National Bureau of Economic Research, women's economic empowerment has a positive impact on the overall well-being of families and communities.

4.  Respectful: Respect is a fundamental quality in any relationship, and a good woman always shows respect towards herself and others. She values other people's opinions and beliefs, even if they differ from her own. A study conducted by the Pew Research Center found that respect is one of the most important qualities in a successful marriage.

5.  Empathetic: Empathy is the ability to understand and share the feelings of others. A good woman demonstrates empathy towards others, allowing her to connect with people on a deeper level. According to research published in the Journal of Personality and Social Psychology, empathy can lead to increased feelings of closeness and social connectedness.

6.  Forgiving: Forgiveness is a key component in any healthy relationship, and a good woman is capable of forgiving others and herself. Forgiveness allows for healing and growth, and it can lead to stronger and more meaningful relationships. According to a study published in the Journal of Positive Psychology, forgiveness is associated with increased life satisfaction and overall well-being.

7.  Responsible: A responsible woman is accountable for her actions and takes ownership of her mistakes. She follows through on her commitments and makes decisions based on what is best for herself and those around her. According to a study published in the Journal of Personality and Social Psychology, responsibility is a critical factor in personal growth and success.

8.  Ambitious: An ambitious woman is driven to succeed and has a clear vision of her goals. She works hard and is willing to put in the effort to achieve her dreams. According to a study conducted by McKinsey & Company, gender-diverse companies are 15% more likely to outperform their peers, highlighting the importance of ambitious women in the workplace.

9. Confident: Confidence is a crucial quality in any aspect of life, and a good woman exudes self-assurance in her abilities and decisions. A confident woman is not afraid to speak her mind and stands up for what she believes in. According to a study published in the Journal of Personality and Social Psychology, confidence is associated with higher levels of happiness and life satisfaction.

10. Supportive: A supportive woman is there for others in times of need, providing encouragement and empathy. She is a source of strength and inspiration, and her presence makes a positive impact on those around her. According to research published in the Journal of Marriage and Family, support is a critical component in maintaining healthy relationships. A supportive woman is able to provide emotional and practical support to those who need it, creating a sense of community and belonging.

Being a good woman is about embodying qualities that foster strong relationships and promote personal growth. From honesty and kindness to ambition and confidence, these characteristics are essential for building a fulfilling and meaningful life. By embodying these traits, women can lead successful and fulfilling lives while making a positive impact on those around them. It's important to remember that being a good woman is not about perfection but rather about striving to be the best version of oneself.

Now sis, when it comes to what men look for in a woman, there are no hard and fast rules. Every individual has their own set of preferences and priorities. However, there are some characteristics that are commonly sought-after by men when it comes to finding a partner. These traits can range from intelligence and kindness to physical attraction and emotional intelligence.

In this section, we will explore some of the commonly sought-after characteristics that men may look for in a woman. It's important to note that these characteristics are not definitive and that every individual's preferences are unique.

1. Intelligence: Many men find intelligence to be an attractive quality in a woman as it indicates her ability to think critically and engage in stimulating conversations.

2. Kindness: Men often look for women who are kind and compassionate towards others as it indicates a caring and empathetic nature.

3. Sense of humor: A good sense of humor can be a major draw for men as it indicates a light-hearted and fun-loving personality.

4. Confidence: Confidence is an attractive quality for both men and women. Men often look for women who are confident in themselves and their abilities.

5. Loyalty: Loyalty is an important characteristic for building trust and commitment in a relationship.

6. Emotional intelligence: Emotional intelligence refers to the ability to understand and manage one's own emotions and those of others. Men may value women who have strong emotional intelligence as it can lead to better communication and understanding in a relationship.

7. Independence: Similar to women, men may find independence to be an attractive quality as it indicates a self-sufficient and driven personality.

8. Physical attraction: Physical attraction is often an initial factor that draws men to women, although it is important to note that physical appearance should not be the only factor considered in a relationship.

9. Honesty: Honesty is an important quality for building trust and respect in a relationship. Men may value women who are honest and upfront with their thoughts and feelings.

10. Similar interests and values: Men may look for women who share similar interests and values as it can create a strong connection and sense of compatibility in a relationship.

# Good Woman (The Checklist)

Choosing a partner is one of the most important decisions you will ever make, and it's crucial to know what you're looking for," says relationship expert John Gottman. When it comes to what men should look for in a woman, there are certain characteristics that can make a relationship more fulfilling and successful. In fact, a study published in the journal Personality and Social Psychology Bulletin found that kindness was the top trait both men and women desired in a long-term partner.

To help you identify what you're looking for, we've put together a checklist of 10 characteristics that men may seek in a woman. Whether you're single and searching, or already in a relationship, this checklist can serve as a guide to finding a partner who is compatible, fulfilling, and satisfying.

1. **Kindness:**

   - Does she actively listen and show genuine interest in what you have to say?

   - Does she demonstrate concern for others, such as family, friends, or even strangers?

   - Does she exhibit emotional intelligence and understanding?

2. **Loyalty:**

   - Does she prioritize trust and faithfulness in her relationships?

   - Does she follow through on her commitments and promises?

   - Does she stand up for you and support you in difficult times?

3. **Emotional Intelligence:**

- Does she express herself clearly and honestly?

- Does she respond well to criticism and feedback?

- Does she understand and manage her own emotions, as well as those of others?

4. **Independence:**

- Does she have her own passions and interests?

- Is she capable of taking care of herself, both financially and emotionally?

- Does she respect and value your independence and autonomy?

5. **Honesty:**

- Does she communicate truthfully and openly?

- Does she take responsibility for her mistakes and shortcomings?

- Does she avoid dishonesty, manipulation, and deceit?

6. **Intelligence:**

- Does she have a curious and open-minded nature?

- Does she enjoy learning and expanding her knowledge?

- Does she engage in thoughtful and stimulating conversations?

7. **Confidence:**

- Does she have a strong sense of self-worth and self-esteem?

- Does she take risks and pursue her goals with courage?

- Does she value and respect herself and others?

8. **Shared Interests and Values:**

- Does she share similar hobbies, passions, and beliefs?

- Does she respect and appreciate your values and interests?

- Does she encourage and support your personal growth and development?

9. **Physical Attraction:**

- Is there a physical chemistry and attraction between you?

- Does she take care of her physical appearance and hygiene?

- Do you feel comfortable and connected with her physically?

10. **Sense of Humor:**

- Does she have a playful and lighthearted personality?

- Does she enjoy joking and teasing in a good-natured way?

- Does she have a positive and upbeat outlook on life?

While these characteristics are not the only factors to consider when choosing a partner, they can serve as a helpful guide in identifying qualities that are important in a good woman. By using this checklist, men can identify potential partners who embody these characteristics and build healthy, fulfilling relationships.

## Exercise 1

Deep Self-Reflection: A Simple Exercise for Personal Development and Growth

Difficulty Level: 8/10

*Introduction:*

Self-reflection is a vital tool for personal development and self-improvement. By taking the time to examine our thoughts, feelings, and actions, we can identify areas where we excel and where we need to improve. In this exercise, we will take a deep look at ourselves and our behaviors to identify areas where we can grow and make positive changes. This exercise is not a replacement for actual therapy, but rather a fun and simple way to promote personal growth and self-improvement.

*Exercise:*

1. Find a quiet and comfortable space where you can be alone with your thoughts. This can be a room in your home or a peaceful outdoor location.

2. Take a few deep breaths and clear your mind of any distractions or stresses.

3. Reflect on your recent interactions with others, such as your friends, family, coworkers, or romantic partner. Think about any conflicts, misunderstandings, or miscommunications that may have occurred.

4. Ask yourself the following questions and answer them honestly:

- Did I listen actively and show genuine interest in what the other person had to say?

- Did I communicate clearly and honestly, or did I withhold information or deceive the other person?

- Did I exhibit empathy and understanding, or did I dismiss or invalidate the other person's feelings?

- Did I take responsibility for my actions and apologize when necessary, or did I blame others or make excuses?

- Did I show appreciation and gratitude for the other person, or did I take them for granted?

5. Identify areas where you can improve your behavior and interactions with others. Write down specific goals and actions you can take to make positive changes.

6. Take action to implement these changes in your daily life. Practice active listening, clear communication, empathy, responsibility, and gratitude in your interactions with others.

Close: Self-reflection is an ongoing process, and it takes time and effort to make positive changes. By regularly examining our thoughts, feelings, and behaviors, we can continue to grow and improve as individuals. Remember, this exercise is not a replacement for actual therapy, and if you are struggling with mental health or relationship issues, it is important to seek professional help. However, this exercise can serve as a valuable tool for promoting personal growth and self-improvement.

# Exercise 2

## Peeling Back the Layers: Uncovering Your True Motivations for Marriage or Commitment

Difficulty Level: 8/10

*Introduction:*

Marriage or commitment is a big decision that requires serious thought and consideration. Many people enter into relationships or pursue marriage without truly understanding their motivations or desires. This exercise will help you peel back the layers of yourself to uncover your true motivations for wanting to be in a committed relationship or get married. It may be a difficult exercise, but the insights you gain will be valuable for making informed decisions about your future.

*Exercise:*

1.  Find a quiet and comfortable space where you can be alone with your thoughts. This can be a room in your home or a peaceful outdoor location.

2.  Take a few deep breaths and clear your mind of any distractions or stresses.

3.  Ask yourself the following questions and answer them honestly:

    •    Why do I want to be in a committed relationship or get married?

    •    What specific benefits do I hope to gain from this commitment?

    •    What fears or insecurities do I have that may be driving my desire for commitment?

    •    Have I examined my own values and beliefs to ensure they align with those of my potential partner?

4.  Reflect on your answers to these questions and consider the following:

- Are my motivations for commitment based on external factors, such as societal expectations or pressure from family and friends?

- Am I seeking commitment as a way to escape loneliness, boredom, or other negative emotions?

- Have I taken the time to explore my own identity and goals independent of a romantic relationship?

- Am I truly ready for the level of commitment and sacrifice that comes with marriage or long-term partnership?

5.  Write down your thoughts and reflections on this exercise, including any insights or realizations you gained.

Peeling back the layers of ourselves is not an easy task, but it is crucial for making informed decisions about our lives and relationships. By understanding our true motivations for seeking commitment, we can avoid making impulsive or ill-informed choices that may lead to dissatisfaction or unhappiness. Remember, this exercise is not a substitute for therapy or professional guidance, and if you are struggling with relationship or mental health issues, it is important to seek help. However, this exercise can serve as a valuable tool for gaining insight and clarity about your own motivations and desires.

# Exercise 3

## Can We Talk?

Purpose: The purpose of this exercise is to promote effective communication within a relationship by determining if the participants have what it takes to navigate difficult conversations.

Difficulty Level: 10

*Instructions:*

1. Choose a topic that is difficult to discuss. It could be something personal or something that has been causing tension in the relationship. For example, discussing financial issues, infidelity, or a disagreement about parenting styles.

2. Set the stage by creating a quiet and comfortable environment with no distractions. Turn off your phones and make sure you have enough time to have a deep conversation.

3. Each person takes turns speaking while the other listens attentively without interrupting or judging. Start with a statement of how you feel about the topic, followed by specific examples and reasons why you feel that way.

4. Use active listening skills to summarize what the other person is saying and check for understanding. Paraphrase what you heard and ask clarifying questions if needed.

5. Avoid blaming, shaming, or attacking the other person. Instead, use "I" statements to express your thoughts and feelings. For example, say "I feel hurt when..." instead of "You always make me feel bad when...".

6. Practice empathy by trying to understand the other person's point of view. Acknowledge their feelings and show that you care about how they feel.

7.  Take breaks if needed, but make sure to come back and continue the conversation until both parties feel heard and understood.

8.  End the conversation by summarizing the main points and agreeing on a plan of action or a compromise. Show appreciation for the other person's willingness to have an open and honest conversation.

9.  Reflect on the conversation afterward and think about what you learned about yourself, the other person, and your relationship. Use this as an opportunity to grow and strengthen your relationship.

Note: This exercise is not easy, and it may take several attempts to master effective communication. Be patient, kind, and supportive of each other throughout the process. Remember that the goal is not to win an argument but to understand and connect with your partner on a deeper level.

# Exercise 4

**Substance or Sex?**

Purpose: The purpose of this exercise is to help individuals make healthy choices when it comes to sex and substance in relationships, specifically when considering marriage and starting a family.

Difficulty Level: 10

*Instructions:*

1. Begin by defining the terms "substance" and "sex" as they pertain to relationships. Substance refers to the deep connection and compatibility between two individuals, while sex refers to the physical act of sexual intimacy.

2. Create a list of characteristics that define substance in a relationship. This could include shared values, mutual respect, trust, communication, emotional support, and the ability to work through conflicts.

3. Create a list of characteristics that define sex in a relationship. This could include physical attraction, sexual chemistry, sexual compatibility, and sexual satisfaction.

4. Reflect on your past relationships and identify which ones were based on substance and which ones were based on sex. Consider what drew you to those relationships and how they made you feel.

5. Think about your current relationship (if applicable) and evaluate whether it is based on substance or sex. Consider how you feel when you are with your partner and whether you share a deep connection beyond physical attraction.

6.  Identify any negative consequences that may come from prioritizing sex over substance in a relationship, such as lack of emotional fulfillment, difficulty in resolving conflicts, and potential for infidelity.

7.  Identify any positive consequences that may come from prioritizing substance over sex in a relationship, such as emotional fulfillment, long-term commitment, and the potential for a healthy, happy family.

8.  Create a plan of action for prioritizing substance over sex in your current or future relationships. This could include setting boundaries, focusing on shared values and goals, improving communication, and seeking therapy or counseling if needed.

9.  Consider discussing your thoughts and feelings with a trusted friend or therapist. They may be able to provide additional insight and support as you navigate this exercise.

Remember that this exercise is designed to help you make healthy choices in your relationships, but it is not meant to be a substitute for professional advice or medical care. If you are struggling with substance abuse or addiction, or if you are experiencing any negative consequences in your relationships, seek help from a qualified professional.

# Exercise 5

## Financial Readiness for Marriage and Parenthood

Purpose: The purpose of this exercise is to help individuals evaluate their financial readiness for marriage and parenthood. It will help them assess their current financial situation, identify areas of improvement, and make informed decisions about whether they are ready to take on the responsibilities of a spouse or parent.

Difficulty Level: 10

*Instructions:*

1. Begin by reviewing your current financial situation, including your income, expenses, debt, savings, and investments. Use a spreadsheet or financial software to organize your finances.

2. Calculate your debt-to-income ratio, which is your total debt divided by your total income. Ideally, your ratio should be less than 36%.

3. Review your credit report and credit score to assess your credit history. Make sure that your credit report is accurate and up-to-date.

4. Identify any financial goals you have for the future, such as buying a home, starting a business, or saving for retirement. Estimate the costs and timeline for achieving these goals.

5. Evaluate your ability to save and budget effectively. Review your spending habits and identify areas where you can cut back on expenses. Create a budget and savings plan to help you achieve your financial goals.

6. Consider the potential financial responsibilities of marriage and parenthood, such as the cost of raising children, healthcare expenses, and the impact of dual incomes on taxes and benefits.

7. Identify any areas of financial weakness or potential risks, such as job instability, lack of insurance coverage, or inadequate emergency savings.

8. Consult with a financial advisor or planner to discuss your financial situation and get professional guidance on improving your finances.

9. Review your progress regularly and make adjustments as needed to stay on track towards your financial goals.

10. Remember that financial readiness is just one aspect of being prepared for marriage and parenthood. It is important to also consider your emotional, physical, and social readiness for these life-changing responsibilities.

This exercise is meant to be challenging, but it will help individuals make informed decisions about their financial readiness for marriage and parenthood. It is important to take the time to assess your financial situation and make any necessary changes to ensure that you are ready to take on these responsibilities.

# Exercise 6

## Emotional Readiness for Step-Parenting

Purpose: The purpose of this exercise is to help individuals evaluate their emotional readiness for step-parenting. It will help them assess their current emotional state, identify areas of improvement, and make informed decisions about whether they are ready to take on the responsibilities of being a stepparent.

Difficulty Level: 10

*Instructions:*

1. Begin by reflecting on your reasons for wanting to become a stepparent. Consider your motivations and how they align with your personal values and goals.

2. Evaluate your emotional state and readiness for step-parenting. Consider your mental health, stress levels, and coping mechanisms. Identify any unresolved emotional issues or trauma that may impact your ability to parent effectively.

3. Research the responsibilities of step-parenting, such as building relationships with stepchildren, co-parenting with the ex-spouse, and managing conflicts within the blended family.

4. Identify any areas of concern or potential challenges that may arise in a blended family, such as differences in parenting styles, loyalty conflicts, or boundary issues.

5. Consider the impact of step-parenting on your current relationships, including your relationship with your partner and your relationship with your own children, if applicable.

6. Develop a plan for building positive relationships with stepchildren, including strategies for establishing trust and respect.

7. Identify resources and support systems for step-parenting, such as support groups, counseling, or books on blended families.

8. Practice self-care and stress-management techniques to help you cope with the challenges of step-parenting.

9. Be willing to communicate openly and honestly with your partner and stepchildren and be open to feedback and constructive criticism.

10. Remember that step-parenting can be a rewarding and fulfilling experience, but it requires patience, dedication, and a willingness to learn and grow as a parent.

This exercise is designed to be challenging, but it will help individuals make informed decisions about their emotional readiness for step-parenting. It is important to take the time to reflect on your emotional state and assess your ability to handle the responsibilities of being a stepparent. With the right mindset, support, and resources, step-parenting can be a positive and enriching experience for both the parent and child.

# Exercise 7

## Stepparenting: Are You Ready for the Challenge?

Stepparenting can be a challenging and rewarding experience, but it's important to assess your mental and emotional readiness before taking on the role. To help with this, consider the following 50 questions.

*Instructions:*

Take the time to reflect on each of these 50 questions to determine if you're mentally and emotionally prepared to be a stepparent. Be honest with yourself as you consider the unique challenges and responsibilities that come with being a stepparent. Consider seeking support and guidance from professionals or support groups if needed.

1. What are your reasons for wanting to become a stepparent?

2. Have you considered the emotional impact of step-parenting on yourself and your family?

3. How do you handle stress and emotional challenges?

4. What coping mechanisms do you use when facing difficult situations?

5. Have you ever experienced trauma or emotional issues that may impact your ability to parent effectively?

6. What is your experience with co-parenting and blended families?

7. Have you researched the responsibilities and challenges of step-parenting?

8. What are your expectations for your role as a stepparent?

9.  Have you discussed your expectations with your partner and their children?

10. How do you plan to build relationships with your stepchildren?

11. Have you considered the unique challenges of building relationships with stepchildren?

12. How do you plan to establish trust and respect with your stepchildren?

13. What strategies do you have for managing conflicts within the blended family?

14. What are your concerns about loyalty conflicts between your partner and their ex-spouse?

15. Have you discussed your concerns with your partner?

16. What is your approach to discipline, and how does it differ from your partner's approach?

17. Have you discussed parenting styles with your partner?

18. How do you plan to handle differences in parenting styles with your partner?

19. What boundaries do you plan to establish within the blended family?

20. Have you considered how your own children (if applicable) may feel about becoming part of a blended family?

21. What strategies do you have for helping your own children adjust to the blended family?

22. How do you plan to communicate with your partner and stepchildren about any issues that arise?

23. Have you identified any potential sources of stress in the blended family?

24.      What strategies do you have for managing stress and preventing burnout?

25.      Have you researched resources and support systems for step-parenting?

26.      Have you considered the financial implications of becoming a stepparent?

27.      Are you emotionally and mentally prepared to take on the responsibilities of a stepparent?

28.      Have you discussed your expectations with your partner's ex-spouse?

29.      What is your approach to co-parenting with your partner's ex-spouse?

30.      What strategies do you have for managing conflicts with your partner's ex-spouse?

31.      Have you discussed boundaries with your partner's ex-spouse?

32.      What are your expectations for communication with your partner's ex-spouse?

33.      How do you plan to handle any negative emotions that may arise when interacting with your partner's ex-spouse?

34.      Have you discussed your parenting philosophy with your partner's ex-spouse?

35.      How do you plan to handle disagreements with your partner's ex-spouse about parenting decisions?

36.      Have you discussed your relationship with your partner's children with their biological parent?

37.      How do you plan to build trust with your partner's children?

38.      What strategies do you have for bonding with your partner's children?

39.      Have you discussed any issues that may arise with your partner's children due to the blended family dynamic?

40.     What is your approach to managing conflicts between your partner's children and your own children (if applicable)?

41.     Have you considered the potential impact of the blended family dynamic on your own children (if applicable)?

42.     What strategies do you have for supporting your own children's emotional well-being during the transition to a blended family?

43.     What are your expectations for communication with your own children about the blended family?

44.     Have you discussed any concerns or fears you may have about becoming a stepparent with your partner?

45.     What strategies do you have for coping with any negative emotions that may arise when dealing with the blended family dynamic?

46.     Have you thought about how you will handle discipline and parenting style differences between you and your partner, as well as with the child's biological parents?

47.     Are you prepared to be patient and understanding as you develop relationships with your stepchild and their biological parents?

48.     Are you willing to seek support and guidance from professionals or support groups if needed?

49.     Have you considered the financial responsibilities that come with being a stepparent, such as supporting the child's education, medical needs, and extracurricular activities?

50.     Do you have a support system in place to help you navigate the challenges that may come with being a stepparent, such as family members, friends, or a therapist?

# Exercise 8

Timing Is Everything: Falling In Love Again

**Purpose:** The purpose of this exercise is to help individuals determine if they are ready to enter into a new romantic relationship after a previous one has ended. This exercise is designed to help prevent individuals from rushing into a new relationship as a way of replacing their former partner, and instead help them make a more thoughtful decision about moving forward.

Difficulty Level: 10

*Instructions:*

1. Begin by reflecting on your previous relationship. Consider why it ended, what you learned from it, and what you are looking for in a new relationship.

2. Consider your current emotional state. Are you still healing from the previous relationship? Do you find yourself comparing your new partner to your previous one?

3. Take a break from dating for a period of time to focus on yourself. Use this time to explore your interests, spend time with friends, and focus on personal growth.

4. Consider seeking professional help or joining a support group to work through any unresolved feelings or trauma from the previous relationship.

5. Before entering into a new relationship, have an honest conversation with yourself about your intentions. Are you looking for a fresh start or are you trying to fill a void left by your previous partner?

6. Be mindful of the pace of the new relationship. Take your time getting to know the new person and avoid rushing into anything too quickly.

7. Pay attention to any red flags or warning signs in the new relationship. Are there any patterns that remind you of your previous relationship?

8. Practice open communication with your new partner. Be honest about your past and your feelings and listen to their perspective as well.

9. Take responsibility for your own happiness and avoid placing too much pressure on the new relationship to fulfill all your emotional needs.

10. Be patient with yourself and the process of falling in love again. Trust that the right person and timing will come when the time is right.

# Exercise 9

**Beyond Settling: Discovering Your True Worth and Pursuing Your Dreams**

Settling in a relationship can be detrimental to one's emotional health and overall well-being. When someone settles, they are sacrificing their happiness and values for the sake of comfort or fear of being alone. This can lead to feelings of resentment, unfulfillment, and frustration in the long run, as the person may realize they are not truly happy in the relationship. Additionally, settling may result in staying in a relationship that is unhealthy or even abusive, which can have serious negative effects on mental and physical health.

For example, let's say Kanye feels that Kim does not treat him with the respect and communication he desires in a relationship, but he continues to stay with her because he is afraid of being alone or believes he cannot find someone better. This would be settling, and it could lead to him feeling unhappy and unfulfilled in the long run. Moreover, if Kim's behavior towards him becomes abusive or detrimental to his emotional well-being, Kanye may continue to stay with her out of fear or a sense of obligation, rather than prioritizing his own safety and happiness. In these scenarios, it is important for individuals to recognize when they are settling and take action to prioritize their own needs and well-being.

Exercise Title: Are You Sure or Are You Settling?

Purpose: The purpose of this exercise is to help individuals evaluate their reasons for entering a relationship and determine whether they are settling for less than they deserve.

Difficulty Level: 10

*Instructions:*

1. Begin by defining what settling means to you. Is it accepting a relationship that is less than ideal? Is it choosing someone who is not your first choice because you fear being alone?

2. Make a list of your non-negotiable qualities in a partner. These are the qualities that you absolutely must have in a relationship. Examples could be honesty, respect, shared values, good communication, and emotional support.

3. Make a list of qualities that you would like in a partner but are not essential. Examples could be physical attractiveness, sense of humor, similar hobbies and interests.

4. Reflect on your past relationships and identify whether you were settling for less than you deserve. Consider why you entered those relationships and whether they met your non-negotiable qualities.

5. Consider your current relationship (if applicable) and evaluate whether you are settling for less than you deserve. Consider whether your partner meets your non-negotiable qualities and whether the relationship is fulfilling.

6. Identify any negative consequences that may come from settling in a relationship, such as lack of emotional fulfillment, resentment, and potential for abuse.

7. Identify any positive consequences that may come from holding out for what you truly want in a relationship, such as emotional fulfillment, mutual respect, and a healthy, happy partnership.

8. Create a plan of action for ensuring that you are not settling in your current or future relationships. This could include setting boundaries, communicating your needs and expectations clearly, and being patient in finding the right partner.

# Exercise 10

**Settling or Thriving? A Checklist for Healthy Relationship Choices**

*Checklist:*

1. Do you feel a deep emotional connection with your partner, or are you just comfortable with them?

2. Are your values and beliefs aligned, or are you compromising on important aspects of your life?

3. Do you communicate openly and honestly with each other, or do you avoid difficult conversations?

4. Are you both committed to growth and personal development, or are you stagnant and complacent in your relationship?

5. Are you physically and emotionally attracted to your partner, or are you just settling for what's available?

6. Do you feel safe and respected in your relationship, or are you being mistreated or abused?

7. Do you share common interests and enjoy spending time together, or do you feel bored and unfulfilled?

8. Are you willing to put in the effort to work through conflicts and challenges together, or do you give up easily and avoid confrontation?

9.  Are you excited about the future and the possibilities of your relationship, or are you resigned to a mediocre or unfulfilling life together?

10. Do you feel empowered and confident in your relationship, or do you feel powerless and trapped?

Use this checklist to evaluate your current or potential relationship and determine whether you are settling for less than you deserve or making healthy choices that will lead to a fulfilling, thriving partnership.

# Exercise 11

**Get Real or Go Home: 100 Hard-Hitting Questions for Relationship Clarity**

*Introduction:*

Before making any significant decisions in a romantic relationship, it is essential to ask yourself and your partner some difficult questions. These questions can be challenging to answer, but it is important to have open and honest conversations to avoid potential trauma and heartbreak. In this exercise, we have compiled 100 true or false questions that you should ask yourself and your partner before agreeing to have sex, get into a relationship, get married, or have a baby. Remember, there is no right or wrong answer, and it is all about what is best for you and your partner.

*True or False Questions:*

1. I am completely over my previous romantic relationships.

2. My partner is completely over their previous romantic relationships.

3. I have been tested for sexually transmitted infections in the past six months.

4. My partner has been tested for sexually transmitted infections in the past six months.

5. I am emotionally stable and capable of handling a serious relationship.

6. My partner is emotionally stable and capable of handling a serious relationship.

7. I have healthy communication skills.

8. My partner has healthy communication skills.

9. I am financially stable and responsible.

10.     My partner is financially stable and responsible.

11.     I have no desire to change my partner.

12.     My partner has no desire to change me.

13.     I feel safe and comfortable around my partner.

14.     My partner feels safe and comfortable around me.

15.     I am comfortable discussing sexual preferences with my partner.

16.     My partner is comfortable discussing sexual preferences with me.

17.     I have a clear understanding of my partner's sexual history.

18.     My partner has a clear understanding of my sexual history.

19.     I am willing to compromise in a relationship.

20.     My partner is willing to compromise in a relationship.

21.     I have similar long-term goals as my partner.

22.     My partner has similar long-term goals as me.

23.     I trust my partner completely.

24.     My partner trusts me completely.

25.     I have met my partner's friends and family.

26.     My partner has met my friends and family.

27.      I am attracted to my partner physically and emotionally.

28.      My partner is attracted to me physically and emotionally.

29.      I am satisfied with my sex life.

30.      My partner is satisfied with our sex life.

31.      I am willing to commit to a monogamous relationship.

32.      My partner is willing to commit to a monogamous relationship.

33.      I am comfortable discussing contraception with my partner.

34.      My partner is comfortable discussing contraception with me.

35.      I have a clear understanding of my partner's religious beliefs.

36.      My partner has a clear understanding of my religious beliefs.

37.      I have a clear understanding of my partner's political beliefs.

38.      My partner has a clear understanding of my political beliefs.

39.      I have a clear understanding of my partner's values.

40.      My partner has a clear understanding of my values.

41.      I am comfortable discussing my past traumas with my partner.

42.      My partner is comfortable discussing their past traumas with me.

43.      I have a clear understanding of my partner's past traumas.

44.     My partner has a clear understanding of my past traumas.

45.     I am willing to work on any issues in the relationship.

46.     My partner is willing to work on any issues in the relationship.

47.     I feel respected and valued by my partner.

48.     My partner feels respected and valued by me.

49.     I am able to express my emotions to my partner.

50.     My partner is able to express their emotions to me.

51.     I am willing to compromise on having children.

52.     My partner is willing to compromise on having children.

53.     I am willing to compromise on my beliefs for the sake of the relationship.

54.     I am willing to relocate to be with my partner.

55.     My partner and I have discussed our future plans and goals.

56.     I am willing to wait to have sex until I feel comfortable and safe with my partner.

57.     My partner and I have discussed our sexual preferences and boundaries.

58.     I trust my partner completely.

59.     My partner and I have discussed how we will handle disagreements and conflicts.

60.     I am willing to make sacrifices for my partner and our relationship.

61. My partner and I have discussed our financial goals and how we plan to achieve them.

62. I am willing to go to therapy or counseling with my partner if needed.

63. I am comfortable discussing my fears and insecurities with my partner.

64. My partner and I have discussed our family backgrounds and how they may impact our relationship.

65. I am willing to communicate openly and honestly with my partner about my thoughts and feelings.

66. My partner and I have discussed our values and beliefs and how they align or differ.

67. I am willing to put in the effort to make our relationship work, even when it's difficult.

68. My partner and I have discussed our expectations for the relationship and where we see it going.

69. I am willing to compromise on non-negotiables for the sake of the relationship.

70. My partner and I have discussed our views on marriage and children.

71. I am comfortable with my partner's past sexual experiences and history.

72. My partner and I have discussed our future living arrangements and preferences.

73. I am willing to work on myself and address any personal issues that may affect our relationship.

74. My partner and I have discussed how we will handle potential long-distance or travel situations.

75.    I am comfortable with the level of emotional intimacy in our relationship.

76.    My partner and I have discussed how we will handle potential infidelity or trust issues.

77.    I am willing to seek professional help if our relationship becomes strained or difficult.

78.    My partner and I have discussed our religious beliefs and how they may impact our relationship.

79.    I am comfortable with the pace of our relationship and not feeling pressured to move too quickly.

80.    My partner and I have discussed our views on gender roles and responsibilities in a relationship.

81.    I am willing to learn and grow with my partner throughout our relationship.

82.    My partner and I have discussed our communication styles and how to effectively communicate with each other.

83.    I am comfortable with my partner's friends and social circle.

84.    My partner and I have discussed how we will handle potential job changes or career shifts.

85.    I am willing to forgive my partner for past mistakes or transgressions.

86.    My partner and I have discussed our preferences for leisure time and how we will spend it together.

87.    I am comfortable with the level of physical intimacy in our relationship.

88.     My partner and I have discussed our expectations for each other's roles and responsibilities in the relationship.

89.     I am willing to respect my partner's boundaries and preferences.

90.     My partner and I have discussed how we will handle potential changes in our physical appearances or health.

91.     I am comfortable with the level of commitment in our relationship and not feeling pressured to commit too soon.

92.     My partner and I have discussed our preferences for pets and how to handle them in our living arrangements.

93.     I am willing to compromise on minor disagreements for the sake of the relationship.

94.     My partner and I have discussed our views on social issues and how they may impact our relationship.

95.     I am comfortable with the level of independence in our relationship.

96.     Are you open and honest about your past experiences with sexually transmitted infections?

97.     Are you willing to get tested for STIs before engaging in sexual activity?

98.     Are you open to using protection during sexual activity?

99.     Are you comfortable discussing sexual preferences and boundaries with your partner?

100.    Are you willing to prioritize consent and respect in all sexual encounters?

# Exercise 12

## The Monogamy Test: Are You Ready to Be Faithful?

*Introduction:*

Monogamy is the practice of being in a committed relationship with one person and being faithful to that person emotionally and physically. In a monogamous relationship, both partners agree to be exclusive and loyal to each other. It is a promise to love, honor, and cherish one another till death do us part.

Infidelity is a major problem in the United States. According to the American Association for Marriage and Family Therapy, 15 percent of wives and 25 percent of husbands have had sex outside of their marriage. Watching pornography is also a form of cheating that can lead to emotional and physical affairs. Cheating can be devastating to the spouse who has been betrayed. It can cause intense emotional pain, damage trust, and can result in the end of a marriage or relationship. Children, family members, friends, and the extended family can all be affected by cheating. It can also contribute to the breakdown of our social fabric, leading to a society with a lack of trust and increased loneliness.

*Instructions:*

This exercise is designed to help you determine if you are ready to be faithful in a monogamous relationship. Answer the following questions honestly and openly. There are no right or wrong answers, but it's important to be truthful with yourself.

1.  Have you ever cheated on a partner before?

2.  Do you have a history of being unfaithful in past relationships?

3.  Are you currently in a committed relationship?

4.  If yes, do you feel emotionally connected to your partner?

5. Do you find yourself frequently attracted to other people while in a relationship?

6. Are you willing to work on your relationship problems with your partner rather than seeking validation elsewhere?

7. Are you willing to communicate openly and honestly with your partner about your feelings and desires?

8. Are you willing to take steps to avoid temptation and create healthy boundaries with others?

9. Are you willing to seek help, such as couples therapy, if your relationship is struggling?

10. Are you willing to commit to being faithful to your partner, both emotionally and physically, for the rest of your life?

Remember, being in a monogamous relationship requires commitment, trust, and communication. It's important to be honest with yourself and your partner about your desires and intentions. If you struggle with being faithful, it's important to seek help and work on yourself before entering into a committed relationship.

# The Monogamy Test II

*Introduction:*

Monogamy is a commitment to be in a romantic relationship with only one partner at a time. It involves emotional and sexual exclusivity, and requires honesty, trust, and communication between partners. Unfortunately, infidelity is a common issue in many relationships, and it can lead to emotional trauma, broken families, and damaged trust. According to statistics, around 20% of married men and 15% of married women admit to having engaged in extramarital affairs. Additionally, the rise of pornography has led to a new form of cheating, where partners may be emotionally invested in or addicted to viewing sexually explicit material, causing emotional and physical distance between them.

*Exercise:*

1. Write down your personal definition of monogamy and what it means to you.

2. List the reasons why you believe being in a monogamous relationship is important.

3. Write about your experiences with infidelity, whether you have cheated or been cheated on. How did it make you feel? What were the consequences?

4. Discuss the impact of pornography on relationships. Have you or your partner ever struggled with pornography addiction? How did it affect your relationship?

5. Write a letter to your partner, expressing your commitment to monogamy and what it means to you.

6. Role-play a scenario where you are tempted to cheat. How would you handle the situation and communicate with your partner?

7. Discuss the importance of forgiveness in relationships. How would you handle a situation where your partner has cheated on you?

8. Research and discuss different types of non-monogamous relationships, such as open relationships or polyamory. What are your thoughts on these types of relationships?

9. Write a list of behaviors and actions that you consider to be forms of cheating.

10. Lastly, write about what you believe is necessary for a successful and fulfilling monogamous relationship, and what steps you can take to maintain it.

Level of difficulty: 10/10. This exercise requires a high level of introspection and self-awareness, as well as a willingness to explore difficult and potentially uncomfortable topics.

# How Ready Am I For A Relationship

Instructions for taking the "How Ready Am I For A Relationship" quiz:

1. Set aside approximately 20-30 minutes of uninterrupted time to take the quiz.

2. Read each question carefully and choose the answer that best describes your thoughts or feelings. There are no right or wrong answers - this quiz is designed to help you reflect on your readiness for a committed relationship.

3. Please answer all 50 questions, as each question is important in assessing your readiness for a committed relationship.

4. Once you have completed the quiz, review your answers, and reflect on what they reveal about your readiness for a committed relationship.

5. Remember that this quiz is only a tool to help you assess your readiness for a committed relationship. It is not a substitute for professional advice or counseling. If you have concerns about your readiness for a committed relationship, please seek the advice of a trained professional.

-------------------------------------------------------------------------

1. What is your main reason for wanting to be in a relationship?
    a.    Loneliness
    b.    Social pressure
    c.    Desire for companionship
    d.    All of the above

2.  How much time do you spend on self-care and personal development?

    a.     Not much

    b.     Some, but not consistently

    c.     Regularly, but not daily

    d.     Every day

3.  Are you willing to compromise in a relationship?

    a.     No, I want things my way

    b.     Sometimes, depending on the situation

    c.     Yes, I am willing to meet halfway

    d.     I am willing to make sacrifices for the relationship

4.  How important is physical attraction to you?

    a.     Extremely important

    b.     Somewhat important

    c.     Not very important

    d.     Not important at all

5.  Do you have any unresolved emotional baggage from past relationships?

    a.     Yes, a lot

    b.     Some, but I'm working on it

    c.     No, I have let go of the past

    d.     I'm not sure

6. How often do you communicate your feelings to your partner?

    a.    Rarely or never

    b.    Sometimes

    c.    Often

    d.    All the time

7. How do you handle conflicts in a relationship?

    a.    Avoid them

    b.    Yell and argue

    c.    Communicate calmly and respectfully

    d.    Give in to avoid conflict

8. Do you have trust issues?

    a.    Yes, I have been betrayed in the past

    b.    Somewhat, but I am working on it

    c.    No, I trust easily

    d.    I'm not sure

9. Are you financially stable?

    a.    Yes, I am financially secure

    b.    Somewhat, but I'm working on it

    c.    No, I have financial problems

    d.    I'm not sure

10. How often do you prioritize your partner's needs over your own?

    a.      Rarely or never

    b.      Sometimes

    c.      Often

    d.      Always

11. How well do you communicate with your partner?

    a.      Poorly

    b.      Somewhat well

    c.      Well

    d.      Exceptionally well

12. How often do you make time for your partner?

    a.      Rarely or never

    b.      Sometimes

    c.      Often

    d.      Always

13. How important is honesty in a relationship?

    a.      Not very important

    b.      Somewhat important

    c.      Very important

    d.      Extremely important

14. Do you have a strong support system outside of your relationship?

    a.    Yes, I have many friends and family members

    b.    Somewhat, but I could use more support

    c.    No, I don't have anyone to rely on

    d.    I'm not sure

15. How well do you handle criticism?

    a.    Poorly

    b.    Somewhat well

    c.    Well

    d.    Exceptionally well

16. Are you comfortable with your own company?

    a.    No, I need constant interaction with others

    b.    Somewhat, but I prefer to be around others

    c.    Yes, I enjoy spending time alone

    d.    I'm not sure

17. Are you able to forgive and move on from mistakes made in the relationship?

    a.    No, I hold grudges

    b.    Sometimes, depending on the mistake

    c.    Yes, I am willing to forgive and move forward

    d.    I'm not sure

18. How important is loyalty in a relationship?

    a.      Not very important

    b.      Somewhat important

    c.      Very important

    d.      Extremely important

19. How often do you make time for hobbies and interests outside of the relationship?

    a.      Rarely or never

    b.      Sometimes

    c.      Often

    d.      Always

20. How comfortable are you with compromising on major life decisions in a relationship?

    a.      Not comfortable at all

    b.      Somewhat comfortable

    c.      Very comfortable

    d.      I'm not sure

21. How often do you initiate intimacy in a relationship?

    a.      Rarely or never

    b.      Sometimes

    c.      Often

    d.      Always

22. Do you feel comfortable being vulnerable with your partner?

    a.      No, I don't like to share my feelings

    b.      Sometimes, depending on the situation

    c.      Yes, I am comfortable being vulnerable

    d.      I'm not sure

23. How important is it for your partner to share your values and beliefs?

    a.      Not very important

    b.      Somewhat important

    c.      Very important

    d.      Extremely important

24. Are you able to admit when you are wrong?

    a.      No, I always have to be right

    b.      Sometimes, depending on the situation

    c.      Yes, I am willing to admit when I am wrong

    d.      I'm not sure

25. How important is it for you to have a partner who is supportive of your goals and aspirations?

    a.      Not very important

    b.      Somewhat important

    c.      Very important

    d.      Extremely important

26. Are you able to maintain a healthy work-life balance in a relationship?

    a.      No, work always comes first

    b.      Sometimes, depending on the situation

    c.      Yes, I prioritize both work and the relationship

    d.      I'm not sure

27. How often do you take responsibility for your actions in a relationship?

    a.      Rarely or never

    b.      Sometimes

    c.      Often

    d.      Always

28. Are you willing to make sacrifices for your partner's happiness?

    a.      No, I am not willing to make sacrifices

    b.      Sometimes, depending on the situation

    c.      Yes, I am willing to make sacrifices for the relationship

    d.      I'm not sure

29. How important is it for you to have open and honest communication in a relationship?

    a.      Not very important

    b.      Somewhat important

    c.      Very important

    d.      Extremely important

30. Are you able to handle long-distance relationships?

    a.      No, I need physical closeness

    b.      Sometimes, but it's difficult

    c.      Yes, I am able to handle long-distance relationships

    d.      I'm not sure

31. How important is it for you to have a partner who shares your hobbies and interests?

    a.      Not very important

    b.      Somewhat important

    c.      Very important

    d.      Extremely important

32. Are you able to give and receive constructive feedback in a relationship?

    a.      No, I don't like to receive feedback

    b.      Sometimes, depending on the situation

    c.      Yes, I am willing to give and receive feedback

    d.      I'm not sure

33. How important is it for you to have a partner who shares your sense of humor?

    a.      Not very important

    b.      Somewhat important

    c.      Very important

    d.      Extremely important

34. Are you able to handle disagreements in a calm and rational manner?

    a.      No, I get angry and emotional

    b.      Sometimes, depending on the situation

    c.      Yes, I am able to handle disagreements calmly

    d.      I'm not sure

35. How important is it for you to have a partner who shares your cultural background?

    a.      Not very important

    b.      Somewhat important

    c.      Very important

    d.      Extremely important

36. Are you able to communicate your boundaries in a relationship?

    a.      No, I have difficulty setting boundaries

    b.      Sometimes, depending on the situation

    c.      Yes, I am able to communicate my boundaries in a relationship

    d.      I'm not sure

37. How important is it for you to have a partner who is financially stable?

    a.      Not very important

    b.      Somewhat important

    c.      Very important

    d.      Extremely important

38. How do you handle conflicts with your partner?

   a.    I avoid them at all costs

   b.    I get defensive and angry

   c.    I try to listen and understand their perspective

   d.    I'm not sure

39. How important is it for you to have a partner who shares your political views?

   a.    Not very important

   b.    Somewhat important

   c.    Very important

   d.    Extremely important

40. How often do you make time for date nights in a relationship?

   a.    Rarely or never

   b.    Sometimes

   c.    Often

   d.    Always

41. How important is it for you to have a partner who shares your religious beliefs?

   a.    Not very important

   b.    Somewhat important

   c.    Very important

   d.    Extremely important

42. Are you able to handle your partner's emotional needs?

    a.    No, I have difficulty dealing with emotions

    b.    Sometimes, depending on the situation

    c.    Yes, I am able to handle my partner's emotional needs

    d.    I'm not sure

43. How important is it for you to have a partner who is supportive of your family and friends?

    a.    Not very important

    b.    Somewhat important

    c.    Very important

    d.    Extremely important

44. How do you handle jealousy in a relationship?

    a.    I become possessive and controlling

    b.    I try to communicate my feelings with my partner

    c.    I ignore it and hope it goes away

    d.    I'm not sure

45. How important is it for you to have a partner who is physically active and health-conscious?

    a.    Not very important

    b.    Somewhat important

    c.    Very important

    d.    Extremely important

46. Are you able to maintain your own identity and interests while in a relationship?

    a.    No, I lose myself in the relationship

    b.    Sometimes, depending on the situation

    c.    Yes, I am able to maintain my own identity and interests

    d.    I'm not sure

47. How important is it for you to have a partner who is willing to compromise?

    a.    Not very important

    b.    Somewhat important

    c.    Very important

    d.    Extremely important

48. How do you handle stress in a relationship?

    a.    I take it out on my partner

    b.    I try to manage it on my own

    c.    I communicate my feelings with my partner

    d.    I'm not sure

49. How important is it for you to have a partner who is spontaneous and adventurous?

    a.    Not very important

    b.    Somewhat important

    c.    Very important

    d.    Extremely important

50. Are you able to trust your partner?

a. No, I have trust issues

b. Sometimes, depending on the situation

c. Yes, I am able to trust my partner

d. I'm not sure

Answer Key for "Am I Ready" Quiz:

| | | | | | |
|---|---|---|---|---|---|
| 1. | b | 18. | d | 35. | a |
| 2. | c | 19. | a | 36. | b |
| 3. | a | 20. | b | 37. | c |
| 4. | b | 21. | c | 38. | c |
| 5. | c | 22. | d | 39. | b |
| 6. | d | 23. | a | 40. | c |
| 7. | a | 24. | b | 41. | c |
| 8. | b | 25. | c | 42. | c |
| 9. | c | 26. | d | 43. | c |
| 10. | d | 27. | a | 44. | b |
| 11. | a | 28. | b | 45. | c |
| 12. | b | 29. | c | 46. | c |
| 13. | c | 30. | d | 47. | c |
| 14. | d | 31. | a | 48. | c |
| 15. | a | 32. | b | 49. | c |
| 16. | b | 33. | c | 50. | c |
| 17. | c | 34. | d | | |

Note:

These are suggested answers and may vary based on the individual's personal beliefs and experiences.

# Ya' Better Call Tyrone

Hey, it's the last exercise, and we're gonna have some fun with it! It's all about Erykah Badu's hit song "Tyrone" from back in '97. We've got some multiple-choice questions for you based on the lyrics of the song. So, read the question stem carefully, then check out the options and pick the one you think is the right answer based on the lyrics. Don't stress too much, just have fun with it! And hey, if you need to sing along to the song while you're doing the exercise, we won't judge.

1. Read the stem of the question carefully. Each question has a stem that contains the main idea or problem being addressed. Take time to read and understand the stem of the question.

2. Analyze the options provided. Each question has four options labeled A, B, C, and D. Analyze each option carefully and consider their relevance to the question.

3. Choose the best answer. Select the option that you believe is the correct answer to the question. Remember to choose only one answer, as multiple answers will not be accepted.

4. Check your answer. Before moving on to the next question, double-check your answer to ensure you have selected the best option.

5. Repeat for each question. Repeat the same process for all the questions until you have answered all the questions.

1.  When you find yourself in a situation in which you are not being treated properly by your partner, who should they contact?

    A.    Jim

    B.    James

    C.    Paul

    D.    Tyrone

2.  Who is the last person to enter your house when your friend comes over to see you?

    A.    Jim

    B.    James

    C.    Paul

    D.    Tyrone

3.  Who is the third wheel on every date?

    A.    Jim

    B.    James

    C.    Paul

    D.    Tyrone

4.  Whenever you think you and your spouse are getting away for some alone time, who is always tagging along?

    A.    Jim

    B.    James

    C.    Paul

    D.    Tyrone

5. Whenever you go out, whose way do you also have to pay, along with your purchase, for both you and your significant other?

    A.    Jim

    B.    James

    C.    Paul

    D.    Tyrone

6. The day you become tired of being taken advantage of and mistreated, who will you tell that deadbeat spouse of yours to contact?

    A.    Jim

    B.    James

    C.    Paul

    D.    Tyrone

7. But he can't use what?

    A. Your curling iron

    B. Your shoehorn

    C. Bottle opener

    D. Phone

8. It has been said that if a person does the work, digs deep into the background of self as well as the people they are considering for relationships, before entering into ill-informed relationships, having unprotected sex, getting into toxic relationships, getting married, divorcing, and aborting unborn children, they will be able to avoid characters like which of the following:

    A. Jim

    B. James

    C. Paul and Tyrone

    D. All of the above

In Lesson 10, we explored the characteristics of a good man and a good woman, and provided checklists to help individuals assess their own qualities and traits. We also included a variety of exercises to help with personal development and growth, including deep self-reflection, uncovering motivations for commitment, discussing important relationship topics, and assessing financial and emotional readiness for various life stages. Additionally, we delved into the unique challenges of stepparenting and provided a self-assessment quiz to determine readiness for a relationship.

Developing healthy relationship skills is essential for building strong and fulfilling connections with others. By understanding the traits of a good partner and assessing our own readiness and motivations for commitment, we can make informed decisions about our relationships. The exercises provided in this lesson offer valuable tools for personal growth and can help us to become more emotionally and financially prepared for the challenges of marriage and parenthood. Stepparenting presents unique challenges, and it's important to be emotionally ready for this role. Overall, this lesson serves as a comprehensive guide to building healthy relationships and making informed decisions about love and commitment.

# EPILOGUE

## WINDING ROAD OF RELATIONSHIPS

Relationships are complex and can often be likened to a winding road, with twists and turns that can be difficult to navigate. When it comes to committed relationships, such as marriage, it's important to have the proper tools and strategies in place to help ensure success. From effective communication to a strong sense of self-awareness, there are several key components that can help individuals prepare for the journey of a committed relationship.

One important tool for navigating the winding road of a committed relationship is effective communication. This includes not only being able to express oneself clearly and honestly, but also being able to actively listen and understand one's partner. Effective communication can help prevent misunderstandings and conflicts and can help foster a deeper sense of intimacy and connection in the relationship.

Another important tool for success in committed relationships is a strong sense of self-awareness. This includes an understanding of one's own needs, desires, and boundaries, as well as an ability to recognize and manage one's own emotions. By developing a strong sense of self-awareness, individuals can better navigate the challenges and conflicts that may arise in a committed relationship, and can better advocate for their own needs and desires.

In addition to effective communication and self-awareness, there are several other tools and strategies that can be useful for those entering into committed relationships. These include developing healthy coping mechanisms for dealing with stress and conflict, cultivating a sense of empathy, and understanding for one's partner, and maintaining a strong support system of friends and family. By having these tools in place, individuals can better navigate the winding road of a committed relationship, and can increase their chances of success and happiness with their partner.

It's also important to recognize that the winding road of a committed relationship is not always smooth, and there may be bumps along the way. However, by having the proper tools and strategies in place, individuals can better navigate these challenges and work towards a stronger, more fulfilling relationship. With effective communication, self-awareness, and a strong support system, individuals can increase their chances of success in the winding road of relationships, marriage, and committed partnerships.

## 7 Key Tools for Navigating the Winding Road of Committed Relationships

Entering into a committed relationship can be a challenging and rewarding experience. While there is no one-size-fits-all approach to navigating the twists and turns of a relationship, there are certain key tools and strategies that can help set the foundation for success. From effective communication to a strong support system, these tools can help individuals build stronger, more fulfilling relationships with their partners.

Whether you are just beginning your journey with a new partner or looking to strengthen your existing relationship, these seven key tools for navigating the winding road of committed relationships can help you build a solid foundation for a happy and healthy future together.

1. Develop effective communication skills: This includes being able to express oneself clearly and honestly, as well as actively listening and understanding one's partner. Effective communication can help prevent misunderstandings and conflicts and can help foster a deeper sense of intimacy and connection in the relationship.

2. Cultivate self-awareness: This involves developing an understanding of one's own needs, desires, and boundaries, as well as recognizing and managing one's own emotions. By developing a strong sense of self-awareness, individuals can better navigate the challenges and conflicts that may arise in a committed relationship.

3. Build healthy coping mechanisms: Stress and conflict are inevitable in any relationship, so it's important to develop healthy ways of coping with these challenges. This can include exercise, meditation, therapy, or other stress-reducing activities.

4. Learn to empathize with your partner: Cultivating a sense of empathy and understanding for one's partner can help build a stronger sense of intimacy and connection in the relationship. This involves being able to see things from your partner's perspective, and to validate their feelings and experiences.

5. Develop a strong support system: Having a strong support system of friends and family can provide much-needed emotional support and guidance during challenging times in the relationship. It's important to cultivate these relationships and maintain a sense of connection with loved ones.

6. Understand the importance of compromise: In any committed relationship, compromise is key. It's important to be able to negotiate and find solutions that work for both partners, even in situations where there may be differing opinions or desires.

7. Take the time to build a strong foundation: Rushing into a committed relationship without taking the time to build a strong foundation can set the relationship up for failure. It's important to take the time to get to know one another, establish trust and connection, and build a solid foundation for the relationship to grow and thrive.

In closing, my goal in this workbook and my manuscript has been to provide you with valuable insights, practical advice, and exercises to help you navigate the ups and downs of relationships. We've explored critical factors that you should consider before entering into a marriage, such as identifying red flags, setting healthy boundaries, and effective communication with your partner. We've also examined the importance of premarital research, investigating your partner's background, and understanding the role of good credit in committed relationships.

My hope is that by using this workbook, you will be well-equipped to make informed decisions about your romantic relationships and set yourself up for success in the future. Whether you are single and looking for love or already in a relationship, this workbook is an invaluable resource for anyone who wants to improve their relationships and live a happier, more fulfilling life.

Thank you for joining me on this journey, and I wish you all the best in your future relationships.

# Answer Key

## Lesson 1: Knowledge Check:

**True or False**
1. True
2. False
3. False
4. True
5. False
6. True
7. True
8. True
9. True
10. False

[Section A, pg. 13 & 14]

## Lesson 1: Knowledge Check:

**Fill in the Blanks**
1. Problems
2. Openly
3. Problems
4. Instincts
5. Boundaries
6. Red Flags
7. Subtle
8. Informed
9. Communication
10. Boundaries

[Section A, pg. 14 & 15]

## Lesson 1: Knowledge Check:

**Multiple Choice**
1. A
2. B
3. B
4. B
5. D
6. B
7. B
8. B
9. B
10. B

[Section B, pg. 19 & 20]

## Lesson 1: Knowledge Check:

**True or False**
1. False
2. False
3. False
4. False
5. True
6. True
7. True
8. True
9. False
10. True

[Section B, pg. 21 & 22]

# Answer Key

### Lesson 1:
### Knowledge Check:

**True or False**
1. False
2. False
3. False
4. True
5. False
6. True
7. False
8. True
9. True
10. True

[Section C, pg. 24]

### Lesson 1:
### Knowledge Check:

**Fill in the Blanks**
1. Boundaries
2. Interrupting
3. Manipulative and coercive
4. Physical
5. Instincts
6. Boundaries
7. Manipulative
8. Communication
9. Jealousy
10. Professional

[Section A, pg. 14 & 15]

### Lesson 2:
### Knowledge Check:

**Multiple Choice**
d. All of the above
b. Inconsistent employment history
c. To protect yourself from potential risks
b. Pretending to be someone else online
b. Investigate further to understand the charges and circumstances
b. Checking for a history of infidelity
d. All of the above
b. Creating fake profiles
a. They may repeat their violent behavior
a. Conducting a background check before the first date

[Section A, pg. 33 & 34]

# Answer Key

### Lesson 2:
### Knowledge Check
True or False
1. True
2. True
3. False
4. True
5. False
6. True
7. False
8. True
9. False
10. True

[Section A,
pg. 41 & 42]

### Lesson 4:
### Knowledge Check
True or False

1. True
2. True
3. True
4. True
5. True
6. True
7. False
8. True
9. True
10. False

[Section A,
pg. 64]

### Lesson 2:
### Knowledge Check:
True or False
1. Ruin
2. Employment
3. Risks
4. Occupation
5. Circumstances
6. Stable
7. Quickly
8. Profiles
9. Violent
10. First

[Section A,
pg. 35 & 36]

### Lesson 3:
### Knowledge Check
True or False
1. True
2. False
3. False
4. True
5. False
6. True
7. False
8. True
9. False
10. True
11. False
12. False
13. True
14. False
15. True
16. True
17. True
18. True
19. True
20. False

[Section A,
pg. 53 & 54]

# Answer Key

## Lesson 5:
### Knowledge Check
**Fill in the Blank**
1. Respect
2. Listening
3. Blame
4. Break
5. Appreciation
6. Name-calling
7. Diffuse
8. Empathy
9. Schedule
10. Environment
11. Never
12. Positive
13. Active
14. Validate
15. Understand
16. Constructive
17. Issue
18. Empathetic
19. Pause
20. Couples

[Section A, pg. 69]



## TYRONE QUIZ
**Multiple Choice**
1. Tyrone
2. Tyrone
3. Tyrone
4. Tyrone
5. Tyrone
6. Tyrone
7. Phone
8. All of the above

[Section A, pg. 181,182 & 183]

**"INCREDIBLE"**

**Audiobook Now Available**

# O'BRYAN
# "GOOD MAN"

# OFFICIAL
# THEME

DIG DEEP
BEFORE
YOU LEAP

DIG DEEP
BEFORE
YOU LEAP

www.digdeepbooks.com

## Available Now Everywhere